Trials of the Visionary Mind

SUNY series in Transpersonal and Humanistic Psychology

Richard D. Mann, Editor

Trials of the Visionary Mind

Spiritual Emergency
and the Renewal Process

John Weir Perry

State University of New York Press

Published by
State University of New York Press, Albany

© 1999 State University of New York

For information, address State University of New York Press,
State University Plaza, Albany, N.Y. 12246

Production by M. R. Mulholland
Marketing by Fran Keneston

Library of Congress Cataloging-in-Publication Data

Perry, John Weir.
    Trials of the visionary mind : spiritual emergency and the renewal process / John Weir Perry.
        p.   cm. — (SUNY series in transpersonal and humanistic psychology)
    Includes bibliographical references (p.   ) and index.
    ISBN 0-7914-3987-9 (hardcover : alk. paper). — ISBN 0-7914-3988-7 (pbk. : alk. paper)
    1. Psychoses.   2. Jungian psychology.   3. Symbolism (Psychology)
4. Self-actualization (Psychology)   I. Title.   II. Series.
RC512.P44   1999
616.89—dc21   98-23483
                                                                          CIP

10   9   8   7   6   5   4   3   2   1

Contents

Preface

While assembling the various papers composing this volume I have been reflecting upon the vicissitudes encountered in the two recent decades in the psychotherapy of acute, disturbing visionary states, commonly considered "psychotic." As I do so, the ups and downs of the sociopolitical climate of those years have given me the same feelings I have known when driving over abruptly rolling hills: when one crosses the crest the momentum lifts one into an exhilarating leap of the heart, only to be followed at the depth of the descent by a heavy sinking sensation of one's inner organs pressing downward. For in the 1970s there was an enthusiastic attitude of openness to new ways and experimental explorations in the mental health field, while in the ultraconservative climate of the '80s funds for such projects were cut off, then in the '90s brains are being treated rather than the psychic life of persons being assisted.

In this sequence of essays the topic of alternative methods for handling acute eruptions of the psyche is treated in a broad range of aspects and challenging considerations.

The thesis here presented is that in many cases the first acute "psychotic" episode should not be considered one of the schizophrenias. If properly received in relationship this experience may even be seen as carrying the capacity to further the growth of the personality. Indeed, in this light the episode appears as nature's way of healing a restricted emotional development and of liberating certain vitally needed functions—in short, a spiritual awakening.

It is natural for the psyche to undergo periods of turmoil, since in order to outgrow a phase of insufficient development and enter a revitalized one, the deep psyche is roused into highly dynamic activity. To remain on an even course, always unshaken by such disruptions, may hold one within the bounds of the statistically normal but it is sure to hold one back from achieving one's full potential, and thus for certain persons is not normal. Some individuals are, by their innate endowment, called upon to escape the bounds of the average and to venture free. If they hold back, the psyche may become so activated as to overwhelm consciousness. When it does so, the state is pronounced abnormal by our culture and moves are made to correct this "decompensation." The psyche, however, has its own aims to pursue in order to fashion a new orientation. The process should not be arrested but allowed to fulfill its own requirements. Such a cooperation with nature's needs, though, requires a new array of attitudes and procedures more nearly aligned with the nature of the psyche's own processes.

This book grows out of a ground of extensive practical work with people in visionary states called acute "psychosis": individual psychotherapy in and out of hospital settings; an experimental research program; and experimental facilities to probe the possibilities of optimal circumstances for fruitful outcomes. Theory, while woven into the fabric of the discussion, is mainly relegated to the volume's second part, since theory is in this effort found to evolve strictly secondarily out of the practical aspects of the work itself.

It is hoped that these several discussions might persuade the reader that certain psychic states, presently treated as acute "psychotic" sickness, should instead be honored as valid operations of the visionary mind playing its rightful part in the spiritual development of individuals and of cultures.

What follows is a list of contents showing where various chapters had their origin, with revisions. 1. Treatment or Therapy: from "Differentiating Psychiatric Treatment and Psychotherapy," a presentation at the University of California Extension Conference, "Psychological Methods in Psychiatry, Monterey, 1990; 2. Thoughts on Thought Disorder: from a paper for a workshop, Taos, 1991; 3. Psychosis or Visionary State?: from "Differentiating Psychosis and Visionary States," a presentation to the Department of Psychiatry, Johns Hopkins University, Baltimore, 1990; 4. Alternative Ways: from "Optimal Circumstances for a Favorable Psychotic Experience," a presentation in a panel of three with R. D. Laing and Loren Mosher, on "Nontraditional Alternatives to Psychiatric Hospitalization," in the Annual Convention of the Maryland Psychological Association, 1997; 5. Transitions in Outlook: from "The Acute Episode as a Transition in Outlook," a presentation at the International Transpersonal Association Conference, Danvers, 1980; 6. Psychological methods: from "Psychological Methods in Psychiatry," a second presentation at the University of California Extension Conference, Monterey, 1990; 7. Jung's Approach: from "Jung and the New Approach to Psychosis," in *Psychological Perspectives*, Spring, 1975, Vol. 6, No, 1, pp. 37–49; 8. Healing Relationship: from "Relationship as Behavior Change in the Psychotherapy of Schizophrenia," in *What Makes Behavior Change Possible?* A. Burton, Ed. New York: Brunner-Mazel, 1976, pp. 304–317; 9. Love and Power in Myth and Ritual: from "Psychosis and the Visionary Mind," in *Journal of Altered States of Consciousness*, Vol. 3, No. 1, 1977, pp.

5–13; 10. Individuality in Myth and Ritual: from "Individuality: A Spiritual Task and Societal Hazard" a presentation at the International Transpersonal Association Conference, Kyoto, 1985, published in *ReVision*, Vol. 8, No. 1, pp. 53–58; 11. Healing in Myth and Ritual: from "World Regeneration and Healing Rites," a presentation at the International Transpersonal Association Conference, Santa Rosa, 1988; 12. Visionary Experience in Myth and Ritual: from "Creativity, Madness and Transformation," a presentation with Joseph Campbell at the University of California Extension Conference on "Ritual and Rapture—Dionysus and the Grateful Dead," San Francisco, 1988; Summary in Respect to Spiritual Emergency: from an article published in *ReVision*, Vol. 8, No. 2, 1980, pp. 33–40; Appendix A. Addendum Queries Following Chapter 8: from "Relationship as Behavior Change in the Psychotherapy of Schizophrenia" in *What Makes Behavior Change Possible?* A. Burton, Ed. New York: Brunner-Mazel, 1976, pp. 304–317; Appendix B. Setting Up a Residence Facility: from a presentation at the University of California Extension Conference, "Psychological Methods in Psychiatry," Monterey, 1990; Appendix C. A Report on Diabasis: from "Alternatives to Hospitalization: Report on Diabasis," presented at the American Psychiatric Association Annual Conference, San Francisco, 1980.

I wish to express my appreciation of the talented assistance given by Phillip Deitch in preparing the early form of the manuscript for this work.

Introduction

In recent years murmurings and complaints are being heard increasingly not only from those who are closest kin to persons undergoing acute "psychotic" episodes, but even among the mental health workers most closely involved with them. Emotional problems and inner concerns are being left to take care of themselves, while treatment regimens are directed almost wholly toward suppression of symptoms. Psychiatry is in a lamentable state when the psyche is in this way being overlooked in favor of measures to improve behavior by the administering of heavy doses of medication.

However, occasional voices are heard now, among those in high places in the psychiatric profession, to say that only when we gain some understanding of the inner life of the "psychotic" person will we be in a position to be of satisfactory help in treating this large population of people suffering this condition.

This volume is addressed to that very issue of penetrating into the workings of the psyche in depth when it is being tossed about by the turbulent upheavals of intense visionary experience. The concern is here solely with the acute episodes commonly called "psychotic," preferably in their first occurrence.

Aside from my private practice in Jungian-oriented psychotherapy, my work over the past forty years in regard to such episodes has been of several kinds: accumulating observations of many cases in individual psychotherapy from the very onset of their acute process; setting up special programs for this work in optimal circumstances; and carrying out extensive investigations in the fields of myth and ritual and of visionary states occurring in the conditions of rapid culture change. At every turn along the way I have encountered, to my surprise, phenomena I did not expect and meanings I had not anticipated.

By good fortune I seem to have been able to recognize certain typical psychic processes and concerns in persons in this particular condition that few in the psychiatric field have discerned. I think this eventuality is due to the fact that in the acute psychic upheaval the preoccupations that assail the individual arise out of the deep unconscious, whose imagery is by nature myth-styled, giving an impression of religious concerns. For professionals whose training and experience have been in psychoanalytically oriented theory and method, such material is not interesting because it finds no place in those frames of thought. For those thoroughly convinced of the appropriateness of the medical model, there is even less place for the acceptance of such "mystical" material into their framework of scientific formulation.

It does not require much digging to unearth the reason for this propensity of mine, since from the very start of my professional education I have been on a quest for an understanding of the psychology of religious phenomena. The particular objective was to learn about a certain psychological function, in the context of an evolutionary framework. I wanted to find the source, in the psyche, of mankind's capacity for loving concern for his fellow beings, that is, a suprapersonal caring that went beyond that for kith and kin, the devotion to one's family and friends, and beyond the bonds of personal love relations. Was this capacity a sublimation of psychosexual drives to ever "higher" levels or did it arise from some other species of motivation? From the start it was clear that the more advanced religions held the development of this capacity to be the prime goal of spiritual cultivation. To achieve a grasp of such motivations required probing into the source of myth and ritual in cultures and into the dreams of individuals. I did not at all expect that the search would at first lead not into the tangled thickets of "psychotic" states in which the deepest layers of the psyche are stirred and laid bare.

Pursuing investigation of psychotic states had certainly not been what I had had in mind, but an event in my residency became the occasion for an abrupt ninety-degree turn into this unexpected direction. Upon my return from training at the C. G. Jung Institute in Zurich, the first case assigned to me was that of a young woman whose inner experience revealed many features hard to comprehend at that time. Her preoccupation with the theme of death and birth I could recognize, and the theme of placing her experience at the center of a quadripartite (a circle divided into four quadrants each with different qualities) image of the world was not unfamiliar; but that an entire process through disintegration into reintegration was represented as proceeding within this symbolic center astounded me. More puzzling was a consistent unfolding in her ideation of political forces that differentiated, then clashed in cosmic-sized cataclysm, finally to resolve into harmony, all exactly timed in synchrony with the clinical states of disturbance and recovery. Yet the feature that I found most intriguing was that throughout her ideation the advent of lovingness onto this symbolic world stage was representing the appearance of a new potential for loving relatedness in her own emotional life. Hers was obviously a spontaneously self-reorganizing and self-healing process. It also afforded a glimpse into the source of that suprapersonal love that I was hoping to probe.

These findings I found sufficiently intriguing to record and enlarge upon in my first book, *The Self in Psychotic Process*,[1] and even to pursue further by volunteering time in inpatient services to work in individual psychotherapy with selected cases during the following decade, the 1950s. Among some two dozen of such experiences I gradually came to recognize a repetitive pattern becoming visible among twelve of them: themes of death and birth, world destruction and creation, clashes of powers whether political or religious or even cosmic, sacred marriages and messianic callings and programs of reform.[2] In each of these the capacity to love was not only a major concern but often the fruit of the turbulent reorganizational process.

The conclusion could not be avoided, then, that the world the person in the episode was experiencing had shifted from the consensual outer reality to this inner myth-styled reality that tends not to be validated in our culture. While I had not heard about this particular image-sequence from Dr. Jung, what I had learned and valued highly was the general therapeutic stance of giving respectful heed to the deep psyche with its images and processes. Since this hidden mind knows more comprehensively than we what is needed for further development and self-fulfillment, we pick up from there the leads for effective therapeutic work. In doing so we learn a firm trust in the capacity of the psyche to discern the way it must take to integrate or reintegrate itself.

Another general guideline I had been given by Dr. Jung was, of course, the method he recommended for an understanding of the psyche's mythic imagery and symbol formation. While the modes of mythic thought and ritual practice were in ancient times the overt expression of psychic concern, they have been left behind by the advances of our materialistic and technological modes of framing our experience, and were thus relegated to "the unconscious." Therefore in order to reach some comprehension of what the psyche's images and symbols signify, we do well to acquaint ourselves with the myth and ritual forms of antiquity. Hence besides recording experiences of many persons in these psychic turmoils, I have found my investigations leading off in a variety of directions and turning up much useful information to serve as means to throw light on the subject.

In the following pages, then, will be found a more recent rounding out of my picture of the self-organizing and self-healing operations of the psyche.

There are two main sections of the book. The first six chapters composing part I deal with the practical issues involved in bringing a psychological view into the actual work of assisting the episodes to reach their fruitful outcome. The second set of six chapters in part II is composed of articles, a few already published, which are pointed toward a more penetrating understanding of the significance of these crises in a framework of depth psychology and evolutionary concerns. An overview succeeds the body of the book in part III as a somewhat all-inclusive statement of the frame of thought that has been explicated, this time seen in the perspective of spiritual emergency.

More specifically, the opening chapter calls attention to several basic premises representing the present-day psychiatric consensus, which can be found faulty when scrutinized from a viewpoint growing out of observations from actual psychotherapeutic experience. The next chapter considers in the same spirit the customary view of the various schizophrenias as "thought disorder," a formulation found faulty if applied to first acute episodes. The third offers the suggestion that if these are viewed as visionary states, there should be some reliable means of differentiation of syndromes indicating which cases should be diverted from the psychiatric regimen and sent to facilities of other kinds. Ensuing upon that question, the fourth makes a fully explicit argument for the advantages of residential facilities as preferred settings for fruitful outcomes of the acute episodes. The fifth renders an account of what is actually encountered in the inner experience during such episodes, the mythic images appearing there reflecting myth and ritual forms effecting transformation of cultures. The last chapter in part I is a practical description of how psychotherapy can be conducted in the most disturbed of such cases and how deep meaningfulness can be discerned in the flow of Ideation.

Part II starts with a seventh chapter that studies the "receptive mode" of orientation called upon in this therapeutic style and exemplified in Dr. Jung's pioneering work and thought. That is followed by an examination of the psychic processes occurring in this interchange between therapist and client in this receptive mode, evoking the image of a psychic Center that directs the development of the self. Chapter 9 shows the role of visionary experience in the reorganization of the psyche both in individuals and in whole societies in times of rapid culture change, and thus in the overall evolution of receptive lovingness in the human community. The next chapter is also given to an evolutionary issue, tracing in history the work of the archetypal Center in various cultures as it fosters the development of individuality. Chapter 11 explores the motif of world destruction and regeneration, or of ritual return to the time of the creation, that occurs in visionary experiences in the healing of individuals and of cultures alike. Chapter 12 examines the interrelations of ecstasy, creativity, and madness in which the realm of death has been considered to be the source of new forms, as seen in the visionary poetry of Shelley and in the cults of Dionysus and Odinn.

In summarizing all these issues, part III recasts them in the framework of spiritual development and cultivation and attendant spiritual emergencies.

There are three appendices: A is an addendum to the eighth chapter; B is a nuts-and-bolts account of how to set up a residence facility for the handling of acute first episodes of visionary states, drawing upon the experience of Diabasis, a residence facility in the 1970s; while C is a demographic study of cases handled at Diabasis.

The reader may well find some of the terms and functions of the psyche quite unfamiliar and therefore difficult to assimilate to a frame of thought more prevalent today. I would do well, then, to explicate beforehand what is meant by these more unusual expressions. Rather than making a full glossary of terms, which tends to be too dry a manner of explanation, I will give a more running account of the term.

The *visionary states* under discussion in this book are the more extreme altered states of consciousness, beyond those marked by mere perceptual changes, and characterized instead by such a degree of activation of the deep psyche that its images flood the field of awareness. The acute first episode of such visionary states, while usually considered "psychotic" in our culture, should be scrupulously distinguished from the chronic conditions known as schizophrenic. In the flooding up of imagery a certain pattern of mythic cast occurs in case after case so regularly as to deserve the term *renewal process*, composed of several transformative operations. The images have an otherworldly quality, numinous and eerie, and are described by Jung as representing the *archetypes* of the collective unconscious. Archetypes themselves are innate predisposition to represent the most typical emotional life experiences in typical symbolic images; they are instinctual and unlearned. When activated, an archetype manifests in the form of an emotion and an image and a pattern of behavior; its charge of energy is intense. I have suggested the term *affect-image* to designate these forms. The *myth and ritual* of all the world's various cultures give expression to these archetypal configurations, and belong together as "things spoken and things done" in religious practices.

Emotion in this model, contrary to psychoanalytic theory, is seen as not belonging to the level of ego-consciousness but rather as autonomous in respect to the ego, that is, acting independently of it, hence being experienced as happening to oneself. *Feeling* is a term reserved for the conscious function of valuation; some emotions may evolve in the developmental process sufficiently to cross the threshold of consciousness as feelings; for example, in love relations, what may start as an involuntary emotion of infatuation may grow into an intentionally espoused devotion, thus a feeling. Emotions come into play in the form of *complexes*; a complex is an emotionally toned grouping or cluster of associations around a nucleus, which is composed both of an archetypal image and of the image of the objects upon which it has been projected; for example, a father complex is composed of all the memories of encounters with the personal father, but contains at its core also the figure of the mythic father. The play of emotions is by this definition the play of *autonomous complexes*.

Among the archetypal images, of paramount importance for an understanding of the renewal process is that which represents itself as a *Center*, whether of one's psyche, or a temple, a city, or even the world as a cosmic axis. Extensive observations of this *central archetype* find it to act as a governing function on any of these levels. Jung has designated this image as representing the archetype of the *Self*. The self-image, then, is encountered on two levels: the personal self-image as who and what one is, and the archetypal self-image as governing what the personality is to become in its self-fulfillment. *Individuation* is, in this framework, the term designating the psyche's innate process leading to self-determination and self-fulfillment. This process occurs on two levels: (1) the growth of one's personality, and (2) an elaborate image sequence constituting the *archetypal individuation process*. The latter involves a play of *opposites* (light-dark, good-bad, order-disorder, cosmos-chaos, life-death, etc.) by which they separate, clash, reconcile, and unite, thus restoring balance and harmony. The archetypal Center stands at this midpoint between opposites, which, when activated, rouse a highly energized dynamic play of image and emotion.

Among these opposites a high-level, all-embracing pair are called in this model *Logos and Eros* (one must put aside for the moment any adherence to Plato's use of the terms). Logos designates a mode that leads to abstracting from the data of experience that which is found relevant to understanding; meaningfulness is found by reflection, which arranges concepts in hierarchical order. In Western cultures Logos is associated with the masculine principle, as our version of the *Yang*. Eros is a mode that leads to entanglement in experience for its own value, thus to enter the web of interrelationships as meaningful in themselves. In Western culture Eros is associated with the feminine principle, as our version of the *Yin*.

Part I

Chapter 1

Treatment or Therapy?

The medical model of handling the acute "psychotic" episode comes under the classification of what is known as "treatment," which implies doing something to the patients to relieve them of their symptoms, even if not to cure them. The alternative paradigm I am proposing is based on a concept of a "therapy" that gives respectful heed to the psychic process underlying the symptoms. The original meaning of the Greek word *therapeia* was a "waiting upon" or "a service done" to the gods, with implications of tending, nurturing, caring, and being an attendant; in time the word was applied to medical care.[1] The original connotation is pertinent to the handling of acute "psychotic" episodes, since the persons undergoing them are in a state of being overwhelmed by images of gods and other mythic elements. Hence a therapist does well to "be an attendant" (*therapeutes*) upon these mythic images so as to foster their work. "Treatment" strives to stop what is happening, while "therapy" attempts to move with the underlying process and help achieve the creative aim implicit in it.

To propose a therapy of this kind in the psychiatric field evokes quite a negative response since it collides with a number of assumptions held in the medical frame of mind. My effort here will be to point out and outline several habits of thought that govern this profession's approach and methodology.

The most prominent of these is the inordinate fear and mistrust of disorder itself. The general consensus holds that the most immediate task is to repair the various mental disorders as rapidly as possible after diagnosis. During routine hospitalization, the staff on the hospital unit become highly upset at disordered behavior and make quick decisions to suppress it, and they feel distinctly reassured when order is maintained and the milieu becomes quiet with the return of normalcy. This behavior may seem perfectly natural and plausible, but an unfortunate consequence of this attitude is that a disintegrative phase of what may be regarded as a developmental process becomes disqualified and ruled out.

Under the alternative model I am proposing, turbulence can be regarded as natural rather than disastrous. Contrary to our general expectations, growth and development do not proceed in a linear and upward fashion, smoothly advancing from point to point like grades in a school, however much we might wish for that. Rather, growth proceeds in a cyclic fashion, with alternating periods of calm and turbulence, progression and regression. Every few years there is an upset in one's experience of the world and a fresh start on a new footing begins. The acute episode we are considering here is another one of these highly charged upsets, but, of course, much more radical in the mode of change and more deeply disturbing. Perhaps only a little less radical than the acute episode is the phenomenon formerly known as "the adolescent storm"; the young person experiencing this state is more usually assessed as a "crazy, mixed-up kid" and the accompanying behavior has remained somewhat allowable, perhaps because "it's just a phase."

The customary imperative to quell turbulence and disorder, as something to repair without delay, is comparable to the way our culture has regarded death. We have viewed death as something to be defeated at all costs and our fear of death has much the same quality as our fear of chaos and disorder, and prompts a similar response. All kinds of inordinate medical technology is brought to bear on the body to keep it alive, even when nature wants to close the book, when it is time for the body to let go of the soul and leave it free to get on to the next thing. But our medical profession is dedicated to fighting death as a dark and dread enemy, just as the psychiatric profession is equally dedicated to overcoming disorder as a similar and fearsome foe.

Now, turmoil and disorder are anything but disastrous if we can actually look into the process giving rise to them. If we listen to the individuals in the episode in an empathetic and caring manner, without the need to manipulate, control, or make them be quieter or different in some way, we find, much to our surprise, that they may change spontaneously in a quite short period of time. We have only to sit and relate openly with persons in the episode to find that what had once been a fragmented state of scattered associations, may now begin to assume a coherent form with clarity of thought. Setting up in this way a bi-personal field of relationship, that is, one in which two psyches are in a process of opening up to each other, may establish an organizing effect that stimulates an integrative process. Fear of disorder or turbulence negates this desirable state, while a sense of open receptivity encourages it.

When we admit individuals who are at the very onset of their acute episode and at the height of their disordered state, they may be fragmented, often mute, with scattered bits of ideation passing across the

mental stage. At this phase of the process the mental content is a hodge-
podge and the ego has quit the field, lost in the deep interiors of the
psyche. Listening to an individual at this time gives kaleidoscopic
glimpses of mythic themes that often leave the listener bewildered. Yet if
we sit quietly and attentively with a person in this state for only two or
three times, we may find the fragments coalescing into a story that
gradually begins to move forward. This development, it is important to
add, is true of most cases, but not all of them.

The initial disordered state that I am describing contains two
distinct elements. The first is an experience of dying or of having already
died, which symbolizes a dissolution of the accustomed self. The second
element, closely related to the first, is a vision of the death of the world.
These "world-destruction fantasies" involve the dissolution of the person's world-image, which symbolizes the accustomed culture or subculture by which the psyche has organized its experience of the world.

Studies of rapid culture change show that the visionary experiences of prophets frequently contain images of the world disintegrating
and being reabsorbed into chaos, which then allows a regeneration to
occur. In these accounts it is clear that what is being transformed is the
image of the culture. We also see this process in the acute episode; one
suffers the collapse of one's accustomed cultural models. One's basic
security and long-held value system, as well as one's view of the world,
are shaken up and disassembled, preparing the way for their recon-
struction. Meanwhile, the psyche remains in a state of inchoate potential.
This process, however, is autonomous and moves naturally into the
reintegrative phase.

A therapist does not have to provide the initiative to move this
sequence forward of make it be something other than it is. Even our
therapeutic interpretations can be minimal, such as simply a lighting up
of the eyes to indicate an acknowledgment and recognition of the import
of the images. The expression of interest has the effect, in itself, of
encouraging the process to move ahead.

Seen in this light, our fearsome "disorder" is merely nature's way of
dismantling what was inadequate in the past, and in so doing allowing a
new start. We would do well to let nature and the psyche do their work in
their own tumultuous way. (Some encouragement for this attitude is
found in the recent recognition of the role of perturbations in processes of
self-organizing systems, as explicated in the works of Jantsch, Prigogine,
and Gleik.)[2]

The second habit of thought prevailing in the mental health field to
which I wish to draw attention is one born of the unfortunate marriage
of psychiatry to the notion of brain disorder as being the prime cause of

"psychotic" episodes—an unfortunate love affair that we hope will be a passing one. Researchers in their various fields who take this view often feel called upon to make a number of expert pronouncements to the effect that we should simply disregard the psychodynamics and psychotherapy that formerly used to draw so much attention, because in their opinion, such approaches have nothing to do with psychosis. In their view, it is to the brain disorder that we must now give our attention.

This perspective presents a most discouraging picture of the future for the individual in the psychotic state, since it suggests that the brain is somehow faulty and will remain forever different from others. Any such judgment can cause severe alienation and stands in need of correction. That frame of thought is based on a mechanistic-causalistic model implicit in biomedical reductionism and represents a philosophic fallacy characteristic of Western thought. Such a model considers anything physical or chemical to be a more fundamental cause than other factors in that it is viewed as being more substantially "real."

In the old language the mind is considered to be a mere epiphenomenon of brain activity and is seen as therefore less real, not lending itself to objective investigation or scientific scrutiny. The psyche's activity is seen thus as quite secondary to the supposedly more basic play of changes at the physical and biochemical levels. Even as late as the 1930s, it was still difficult for our profession to accept the premise of psychosomatic medicine,[3] asserting that the psyche's problems and disturbances could produce effects in the internal organs of the body. A little later this formulation was accepted, but only for certain syndromes such as ulcers, hypertension, and asthma, which were considered to be exceptions to the general premise that etiology was primarily the province of biochemistry and physiology.

Reductionistic assumptions such as these overlook the obvious observation that the parts of the organism move together as a whole. Psyche and soma, with their attendant emotions, physiology, anatomy, and chemistry all operate simultaneously in coordination with each other and the whole. To say that the part is prior to the whole, in a causative sense, is to lose any sense of the wholeness of the organism. This is especially true in regard to the emotions. In rage, fear, love, or grief, the physiology changes in ways specific to each, yet one cannot therefore say that the anger or grief reaction is caused by the chemistry! The reality is simply that the biochemical processes participate in the total experience of each emotional state. The biochemistry is not a cause but a concomitant. If this is so in regard to ordinary emotional states, it must especially be the case in turmoils as severe as acute psychosis. (Engel has made an eloquent appeal for recognition of the need for a new mode of conceptualizing that embraces all levels of experience of the organism, recommending his biopsychosocial model.[4]

The question of a genetic factor in the formation of the brain that produces a proclivity to psychosis is also part of this same issue of causation. Some current researchers hold to the idea that the effect of the gene currently under scrutiny is one that conveys an inclination toward extrasensitivity as opposed to pathology; if this is so, it would fit the psychological observations much better. The individuals most apt to undergo an episode of the kind we are examining are usually endowed with a highly sensitive makeup, so that in childhood they were inclined to perceive falseness, defensiveness, and hidden emotions more than others. The perception of such characteristics is usually, of course, less than welcome in a family accustomed to denial. These sensitive individuals accordingly were made to feel in an awkward position because they perceived what others did not and hence they were made to feel odd or wrongheaded, resulting in a sense of being excluded from the oneness of the family circle and cast in the role of the family scapegoat. These and other points have been extensively pursued and documented very tellingly in the work of Laing and Esterson in *Sanity, Madness and the Family*.[5]

The best evidence for the proposition that the "psychotic" state cannot rest upon faulty anatomy, physiology, or brain chemistry is the readiness for the syndrome to clear up even during a single interview, at least for a time. One may sit with a person enveloped in the psychotic state and reach a point of good rapport, allowing an open connection to be reached in the relationship between the two persons involved, and also between the individual and the underlying psychic process. In such conditions the psychotic state may abruptly clear up. There can occur, then and there, a return to coherency and clarity of thought, and the so-called "thought disorder" can melt away. This change may last for a few hours or even a few days and then the individual may slip back into his or her former psychotic mode, or the coherent state might, with good fortune, persist. After such experiences as these it is increasingly difficult to conceive of a brain or biochemical disorder as being the primary causative agent of such states. A further corroboration of this point is the occurrence of rapid change from a psychotic condition in clients in only one to three days. This change occurs very frequently with no medication needed to bring this about, when the setting is favorable.

A third habit of thought in the psychiatric profession I would like to cite involves an issue quite close to those previously discussed: it concerns the nature and role of emotion, a subject that has been fraught with controversy since the beginnings of psychology. Since the late nineteenth century emotion has been considered a "disorganizational response," a view borne out by such tests as the recording of hand tremors before an ordeal such as an examination, demonstrating on a graph that emotions interfered with normative functioning. An informative review of the history of such unfavorable attitudes toward emotion in academic psychology has been written by Leeper.[6] In the cognitive therapy school of Ellis and others[7] emotion is regarded as an unnecessary mode of behavior that is best examined with rational criticism rather than being expressed. The same attitude is prevalent among those treating psychosis. Emotions are viewed as constantly threatening to be out of hand and when they are stirred up matters are handled rigorously to prevent disturbance. There results an inclination to keep the emotions suppressed in order to maintain an atmosphere of calm and quiet as well as a general sense of order among the patient community and hospital staff.

The episodes under consideration here come under the diagnostic category of "thought disorder," implying a tendency toward concreteness of thought and impaired ability to abstract. However, we find in therapeutic work that the more fundamental problem is an impairment of the affect, which is often found to be flat, blunted, or at least inappropriate. As soon, though, as we can establish a good therapeutic relationship with an individual in a psychotic state, we find that the affect begins to act more naturally. Indeed, part of the healing process consists of getting the affect to move and be more vivid.

In the "high arousal state"[8] that is, when the deep psyche is highly activated in the "psychotic" episode, the colorful mythic images are representations of core emotional issues. In the normative state, images are part of the nature of emotion and consequently image and affect operate hand in hand with each other. An image renders the meaning of an emotion, and the emotion gives the image its dynamic. In the "extreme altered states" (in the acute "psychoses"), this connection tends to fall asunder, producing one of the foremost "splittings" formulated by Bleuler and causing him to name the syndrome "schizophrenia" ("splitting of the mind").[9] A result of this "splitting" is the phenomenon of images floating through the field of awareness without coherent connection to the emotions that would in the normative state naturally belong to them. An example of this would be a person speaking of the collapse of the familiar world as if it were no more alarming than saying that the market will be closed tomorrow. In this fashion frightening and utterly horrendous world and cosmic events are portrayed without fear, and in listening we are left with an almost inanimate picture of them. Emotional expression is designed for communication and therefore, in the therapeutic model I am proposing, it is the communication in the therapeutic relationship that allows the affect to be restored to the image.

This restoration is particularly desirable in regard to the more problematic emotions and the conflicts associated with them, the angry and sexual ones being the two of greatest concern. These emotions frighten staff members in hospital settings more than any other and call for the greatest degree of suppression in the name of law and order, yet these are the emotions most needed for the future growth and development of the personality.

Anger is essentially the raw, root material out of which evolves an assertiveness most needed by a weakened ego, and sexual emotions are the ground out of which evolves a capacity for an intimate and caring relatedness to others. This sense of bonding is vital for those individuals who have typically evaded closeness because of the fear of being hurt. The acute episode aims to liberate both these affects and yet the law-and-order orientation in our present-day hospital system prevents the very process that nature is attempting.

An example of this may be seen in the case of a resident I once supervised who had charge of a young man who, in giving vent to his rage, started breaking the hospital furniture and had to be confined to his room. The staff were made understandably anxious and became intolerant of his behavior. He was considered unmanageable and the plan was to have him sent on to the state hospital. I advised the resident to sit with him for as long as possible and hear what his anger was about, and thus get to the issue more directly. The man ranted for an hour or two in a long and wearing session, but in this way the underlying issue was actually reached and he was able to quiet down of his own choice. The result was that he remained in the hospital instead of being transferred.

In my experimental projects we have set up a "rage room" as a safe place to let fly with whatever needed to come up into expression. If a client were cutting up excessively and had to work off the anger, we would invite him or her to this place, where the walls were soundproofed and cushioned, as well as the floor. Cartons and other expendable objects could be beaten up, boffer swords could be swung, and a life-sized punching bag attacked. This room became a favorite place to frequent and had a meaning opposite to that of the conventional "seclusion" room, where someone would be locked alone behind steel doors with only a little window to peer through. In the "rage room" a staff member would accompany the client inside, hear, and even receive the rage, and together they would find the meaning of it. This experience has been very powerful and highly therapeutic.

Issues involving sexual emotions are no less difficult for a hospital staff to handle. We had a young woman client in our residence facility (Diabasis), in her late twenties, who was married, a mother of two, but whose marriage was in difficulty. Our experience with this woman raised a number of problems around sexual issues that represented themselves in her initial identification with what, in her words, she described as the "Love Goddess." She was so constantly seductive with the male staff members that they were made anxious and somewhat intolerant of her behavior.

She came with the conviction that she was dying and that her god was a plant that was withering and dying. She felt herself to be in the Garden of Eden as a little girl. She was solidly identified with what she described as the "Goddess of Love" herself. She saw a "War of the Worlds" threatening the destruction of our world by earthquake, flood, and fire, as an apocalypse that would usher in a "New Era" for mankind with the "Coming of the Lord" from outer space as a new messiah. Her spiritual calling, she knew, was to prepare the world for this great event. The spiritual rebirth arising out of her initial death experience she envisioned as tender green shoots growing out of the withered divine plant, calling them her "new reborn feelings." This line of thought was no mere chatter: she was picturing actual events in her psychic life, namely her awareness of her new capacity for relating to people with more caring. This warm feeling amounted to a differentiation of the potential for lovingness from its archaic state in identification with the "Love Goddess." She was indeed entering a new state of her inner world after abandoning the old one.

Within a month she began perceiving that she was not actually relating or even listening well to other people and thus not allowing them to connect with her. The love she had spoken of was merely an archetypal image of love, personified in the deity and felt only in its cosmic dimension, full of a vast potential but by no means actualized or personalized. Any component of one's development, such as love, first appears in an archetypal form as a potential and motivation for certain functions. The inchoate potential evolves step by step through a number of concrete experiences into a capacity for intimacy and a caring relatedness with others. By the end of a few weeks this young woman's feeling was no longer showing itself as sexual playfulness but rather as real human warmth.

For someone in the acute "psychotic" episode it is essential to go through this differentiation of the Eros principle[10] and it must not be opposed, inhibited, or stopped. Our staff at Diabasis were selected on the basis of their being caring individuals who would be open with each other and form an affectionate community, and in this way model for our clients a way of living in relatedness.

The fourth habit of thought that I would like to consider concerns the negation of the existence of an inner life. A large proportion of our profession, as well as others in the mental health field, are heavily influenced by the behaviorist school of psychology as well as one of its major derivatives, behavior modification. Even more are under the sway of the various schools of psychoanalytic thought, some of which still hold to a biologically based framework of drives and their prohibitions, sublimations and vicissitudes, a model in which the unconscious is, in large part, derived from repressions. In such circles the mention of an inner spiritual life, with its own requirements to foster its inner processes, evokes little recognition and is apt to be quietly dismissed as too mystical.

These views of the psyche, postulating that it can have no internal life of its own in depth, no inner world developing by its own quite different modes, represents a philosophic bias that has dominated our thinking about the psyche since the seventeenth century. This view was expressed by John Locke, who stated the proposition that we come into the world with a mind that is a blank slate or "tabula rasa."[11] What we come to be is then the creation of our experience, composed of the input of our senses, thus allowing the conclusion that there is nothing in the mind that has not come through the senses from outside.

One of the most influential expressions of this quite negative view of the deep psyche is Silvano Arieti's *Interpretation of Schizophrenia*.[12] In this work he portrays schizophrenia as an "escape from reality" through the mechanisms by which the patient attempts to "envision reality in a less frightening manner," that is, when his defenses become increasingly inadequate. These defenses are "mechanisms which were used by the human race in the process of becoming the species that it is today. In other words they are obsolete, archaic mechanisms, buried long ago in unconscious processes." Arieti speaks here of psychiatric conditions in which one finds "the use of less evolved mechanisms for functions which require higher processes. These bring about peculiar situations," he states, "that have never occurred normally in previous stages of phylogenesis." This may reinforce the point that some interpretations are "nothing less than phylogenetic fantasies." He further believes that "it would be nothing more than phantasy to explain phylogenetically the dynamics of a single state of schizophrenia. . . . This is the mistake Jung made. Jung thought the collective unconscious could explain the motivations of the individual. This is not the case." He states that "to understand the formal or psycho-structural aspect of a psychiatric condition we must transcend the ontogenetic level." In these statements Arieti grants little value to the work of the archaic, myth-styled images in the process of psychic reintegration, which according to his view, must come from a higher structural level better oriented to outer reality. In that model the higher structural level is the synthetic function of the ego as defined by psychoanalytic theory. Yet the reintegrative process that we have seen is in no way being performed by the ego, which, if anything, remains in a state of disintegration until the process has been completed.

With the bias that there is no inner spiritual life with a purpose of its own, there would be no place for the spontaneous and autonomous inner processes in depth, particularly those of a self-healing nature. Yet it is just those processes that we see in the acute episode so regularly that they appear to be predictable: a sequence of images recurring in case after case, representing the moves of an inner life going on quite independently toward their own goal. If in listening to this process we get in the way, it proceeds regardless and pushes us aside in order to move ahead, and if we are not receptive to certain levels of this development, there is a tacit response, that if verbalized would be: "To hell with you, I'm not going to tell you much!" There then ensues a withdrawal, leaving the listener in a position of never hearing what is taking place in the individual. On the other hand, if our face lights up to what is being communicated, with a sense of recognition of its import, then in doing so we may find a whole wealth of material pouring out that we would have never even guessed was there.

In my view, it is the existence of this inner life, with its own process of reintegration through disintegration (in much the same sense as the process studied by Dabrowski)[13] that provides the principal justification for the regimen of psychotherapy without medication in a residence facility. Naturally, it is more humane to have a homelike setting for handling the acute episode, one not regimented in a law-and-order atmosphere; that quality alone would make it beneficial. Yet of far more importance is the arrangement of an environment in which nature is allowed to proceed with its self-healing processes, designed to give them full acknowledgment and affirmation. If the facility were not aimed at this purpose, the entire concept would be far less convincing.

In addition to Diabasis two projects in the San Francisco Bay Area have demonstrated the advantages of regimens that did not rely on the use of medication: the Agnew Project,[14] which was not residential, but showed the patients doing better without medication by a ratio of nine to one; and Soteria House,[15] which was residential but did not emphasize relating to the inner self-reorganizing process.

In speaking of the acute episode as a self-healing process, we are confronted with what at first appears to be a paradox for those who think in terms of psychopathology. If the acute episode is a psychosis, then it must, by definition, be disorder, and how can a disorder be healing? Also, if there is no disorder, then what is there to be healed? In my view the "disorder" lies in the so-called prepsychotic personality, that is, in the insufficient emotional life of the individual up to the time of the first break, the emotional aspect of development having been severely limited and inhibited. For these individuals the interchange of feeling has been considered unsafe and intimacy seen as threatening. In many ways their experience has shown that feeling cannot be afforded because of the danger of being hurt. The residence facility is designed to be a safe environment for the expression of emotional intimacy and for the full expression of feelings of any kind, especially warmth; all the various emotions can be released as well as acted upon and responded to. This element has shown itself to be an essential part of the healing process.

A fifth habit of mind that needs to be reckoned with is the preference in our culture for the "quick fix," by which we are inclined to demand of any procedure that it be short, fast, and therefore inexpensive. The medication regimen fits this expectation so well that in the average psychiatric facility the pressure is aimed at having any new case "stabilized" within a week and quickly discharged; if by the middle of the next week this development has not occurred, the staff begin to ask what the problem is and the dosage of medication is increased.

The reason for this haste is, of course, economic: mental health boards and hospital administrations are pressed in this direction by the circumstance that the budgets are drawn up annually, and under various stringencies the allotments are usually cut back each time. Hence if one draws up a detailed five-year trajectory, demonstrating that in the long run considerable money is saved by alternative methods, this proposal falls on deaf ears because of the preoccupation with budgets designed for one year at a time. The conventional sequence of acute care, aftercare, continuing OPD visits with medication adjustments, plus board-and-care costs, all on top of adding one more person each time to the population of minimally capable persons dependent on the county, all mounts up to a huge expense. If the acute episode can be self-healing, why not take advantage of this process and benefit from it?

Now it appears that nature, not being budget-minded, has long since arranged that visionary experiences of various kinds, including acute episodes, have a tendency to take six weeks to accomplish their inner aims. It is intriguing to reflect on the connotations of this, for the number is recognizable as forty days, with all this time's connotations: the biblical accounts of the visions of Esdras,[16] Jesus's forty days in the wilderness,[17] or the world-destruction imagery of the Deluge,[18] all conform to this pattern. Also to these examples can be added the contemporary programs of autogenic training, language learning, and brain washing, all of which are geared to a six-week threshold to take effect. There appears to be something in the programming of the psychic organism that is designed in this particular way. Pacing is an important phenomenon that invites our scrutiny. Our experience indicates that in the acute episode the more floridly disturbed the persons are, the more rapidly they move through it. Intensity seems to correlate directly with brevity of time, and with favorable outcome. The persons who are frightened, overwhelmed with imagery, and engrossed in their preoccupations are the ones most likely to have a favorable inner experience, from which they emerge with significant change.[19]

At Diabasis we had no little tremor of misgiving when we were told to set the limit of stay to two months, but we found this to be enough time for the live-in segment of the clients' involvement with us. We added to this then an offer of a third month of daytime stay in a second house in the same circumstances as the first two months, and then again an offer of another six months of regular interviews with the same staff member as before. We joked about this, that it was perhaps not entirely accidental that this time period added up to a nine-month process of being delivered into the world anew!

I cite these several habits of mind in the psychiatric profession and the mental health field in general in order to point out that alternative methods and programs are based upon premises entirely different from those governing our present-day conventional practices. When funding is sought for new alternative ventures in the future, considerable clarity about the differences in presuppositions is imperative. Even more striking among the efforts on the part of psychiatrists to understand psychosis is the persistent pursuit of a principal feature of that syndrome, a disorder of the thinking process, which now calls for our attention.

Chapter 2

Thoughts on Thought Disorder

Although there is some consensus in psychiatry that schizophrenia is thought disorder, there are so many differing and contrasting formulations of it that we need to reflect about the relativity of psychological conclusions.

In our Western culture, as individuality increases so does diversity grow to such an extent that we find ourselves living in different universes. Outwardly we might seem to look and act somewhat the same in some measure, but when we allow ourselves to be seen at a deeper level and reveal our belief system, our value system and our lifestyle preferences, we find ourselves living by almost as many subcultures as there are persons.

Compare our times to the medieval era, for example. The sociologist Sorokin, in his exhaustive study of the cycles of cultures,[1] defined an "ideal" type, such as occurred in the Middle Ages in which a unitary structure of faith and ethics, and of hierarchical political and religious institutions, prevailed. In contrast to such a consensus that gave the spiritual dimension the highest value, our modern era since the Renaissance has granted the highest honor to the achievement of individualism and to an outlook that establishes materialism as the framework of our philosophy of "the good." In this type of culture, called by Sorokin "sensate," the "abundant life," which used to convey the implications of spiritual enrichment, has come to signify the acquisition of things.

In this trend from unity to diversity we find truth becoming increasingly relative. We live by differing truths. Does this imply that truth is illusory and futile to seek? A difficult point for many to grasp is that it is the task of each and all of us to find our own truth, even though consensus may not make its appearance to reassure us.

To be creative is to be original, and to achieve one's unique individuality is a creative work. As we grow into self-fulfillment we become increasingly idiosyncratic. An accomplished individual becomes in some degree an anomaly!

Surely, one might object, science seeks truth and builds up a more and more realistic definition of nature, and thus gradually reaches a true rendering of it. Yet the more we familiarize ourselves with the history of science and its theories, the more we recognize that science is a creative work and that the most creative scientists are accordingly original by disposition. One of the more exciting features of science is the contention that occurs over differing conclusions, always striving toward a truth that is always elusive in the end.

This particular feature is most startlingly and distressingly evident in the field of psychology. We find it to be a discipline that is as polyglot as can be, with as many theories of personality and mental process as there are psychologists. Every major school of thought among the dozens is different, all viewing human nature in their own way and all contradicting each other. To some this might seem bewildering and appalling, while to others it makes the search for a true theory all the more intriguing. The conclusion that finally becomes unavoidable is that each psychology, each school, is an expression of the personal makeup and standpoint of its originator.[2]

Yet the creative originator's personality is only one among the factors giving shape to a psychology. Influence on a more general level comes from movements and trends of the culture in any particular decade, becoming reflected in the prevailing frame of thought. This is true not only of psychiatric formulations, but surprisingly pertains even to the very incidence of certain syndromes in psychopathology itself. Studies of records[3] have shown that among the "schizophrenias" there was a high rate of occurrence of catatonic types in the 1920s and 1930s, which then dropped off in succeeding decades to the point of rarity at present. In the postwar period of the 1950s what could be a more natural expression of the temper of the culture than the sharp rise that occurred in the diagnosis of paranoid types? Then came the era of the 1960s with its counterculture and its widespread recognition of the phenomena of altered states of consciousness, especially in the wake of the popular use of psychedelics and meditative techniques. During that and the next decade the most common form of psychosis was the syndrome at that time called "acute undifferentiated schizophrenia," in which the deep psyche seemed to be opening up so fully as to seem inside out! In another clinical arena, that of the neuroses, hysteria of the conversion type had been in the early decades of this century very common and a subject of much psychiatric scrutiny; it dwindled away to such an extent that it is now quite rare except in certain immigrant populations from other cultures.

Attitudes on the part of the psychiatric profession also have shifted remarkably from decade to decade. I have been privileged to watch these changes through a span of five decades, the most striking being the '60s. With the rise and prevalence of the counterculture in the middle of that decade, the psychiatric residents whom I was teaching and supervising suddenly changed in manner and appearance with beards, bellbottoms, and beads, all to the delight of their patients. These were heard to exclaim, "This is wonderful! We can really talk to these doctors now!" The destiny of residence facilities as alternatives to hospitalization without medication also reflected the tenor of the times. In 1970 the National Institute of Mental Health (NIMH) was funding experimental research programs such as ours at the Agnew Project to determine who did well without medications. The Diabasis program was made part of San Francisco's Mental Health System in 1973, but met political opposition that closed it. Upon reopening after two years, we were given the status of facility of choice for the acute first episodes in the county's mental health system. In another two years' time the county's policies recoiled radically into an ultraconservative stand, and although we were decidedly successful and well regarded, we were abruptly cut off from county funding along with all other special services (leaving only two crisis units). Of course, in the ultraconservative 1980s any thought of carrying out such a project became unthinkable.

Although this history of those decades is familiar enough, I am retracing it here in order to make a point about the nature of psychological theories and models. A piece of experimental research or a treatment approach does not lead to a conclusion or formulation that stands by itself as objectively validated "truth." Rather it should be viewed as a special instance in the context of an entire cultural configuration, as a part in the whole of a cultural set. This societal whole governs in great measure what the part becomes. A psychological formulation seen from this perspective needs to be evaluated in terms of the question whether the investigator is representative of forward-moving trends or of established views about to wane into the background. This suggestion, of course, does not imply that almost anything new is to be valued highly for its newness, although in our rapidly progressing culture this seems to be a habitual tendency. Rather, what is concerned is the deeper issue of whether the new statement participates in the current thrust of a culture pressing on toward ever increasing levels of understanding. Freud was firmly rooted in the scientific framework of the nineteenth century and spoke in terms readily understandable to the profession of his later years. Jung's explorations were motivated by a number of interests that became prevalent only toward the latter part of this century. J. B. Rhine's findings in extrasensory perception[4] were totally unacceptable to the psychological profession of the 1930s, yet they gradually have been granted more general recognition.

In these comments I have been alluding to the fields of psychology and psychotherapy in general, but when it comes to the problem of understanding the "schizophrenias" specifically, the issues need even more urgently to be recognized. I stress this because in the last decade it has become apparent that the negative attitudes toward this condition on the part of the profession have a strong effect on what the condition actually becomes. If, on the other hand, a therapist relates to the thought and behavior as meaningful and representing a crisis in growth and development and the individual feels validated, the psychotic state may then clear up within a quite short time. In recent decades the role of the observer in scientific investigation is being increasingly recognized as playing a part in the process that is being scrutinized; psychiatry would do well to heed the point.

It has become customary for clinicians to lump together the several phases and various types of schizophrenia under the general designation "thought disorder." This way of viewing the condition overlooks an observation recognized for several decades, namely that the phenomena in the thought disorder category of symptomatology are not seen in the first acute episode, or only rarely.[5] Yet in San Francisco in 1979 the statistical data-gathering did not even differentiate first episodes from later ones, or acute from chronic!

To clarify the terms under discussion, it must be borne in mind that the term *thought disorder* does not refer to the content of the person's communications. The content is called "ideation," which in the descriptions of the schizophrenias is called "*bizarre* ideation," signifying ideation that is unusual and not understood. What we are concerned with now is "formal thought disorder," signifying certain measurable traits that the communication of thought reveals in its form. There is considerable literature on the topic that would take an entire volume to review, and I will comment only on certain highlights of the formulations.

In the various renditions of the topic, it becomes apparent that each springs from an underlying paradigm that is concerned with how the psychic organism operates, and each reveals the investigator's outlook and view of human nature. There are spokespersons for the more mechanistic framework who find a faulty conceptualizing function, as if it were a damaged tool. On the part of many there is a strong conviction in predicating a "brain disorder," which reflects the prevailing preference for the view that what is physical and chemical is necessarily primary in causation. Then we find systems theory making its mark in pointing to the levels of the general functioning of the total organism as revealing faultiness, rather than the functioning of the parts. There are those who study the errors in logic and find a "paleological level" reached in a gradual retreat from a harsh and frightening reality.

It has been generally held that the principal feature of "thought disorder" is a deficiency in the capacity for abstraction, accompanied by its counterpart, a tendency to understand and express ideas only on a concrete level. This formal "thought disorder," amounting to an object-bound state, is most pronounced in true "schizophrenia" (this term is reserved for a condition lasting at least six months, during which there is a downhill advance of disintegration and deterioration). It is least pronounced in the first acute episodes, the very ones that patients are the most apt to recover from. These early episodes are defined by their duration: if four weeks or less they are "brief psychotic disorder"; if lasting two months, "schizophreniform disorder." This kind of categorizing according to time rather than to the nature of the psychic process is unfortunate but at least leaves room for the claim that the first episodes are not necessarily schizophrenic and should not be called so until half a year goes by.

I will epitomize very briefly some of the salient features of the "thought disorder," as formulated by Goldstein and his contemporaries,[6] in order to compare their general viewpoint with the one that I am advocating. (I have concluded that more recent studies on the topic have become of little value since all subjects of this category are by necessity medicated, thus invalidating the findings.) The picture presented is that both abstract and concrete behaviors are expressions of the total personality, not specific aptitudes. There are changes in the total behavior, of which thinking is only one special expression. Thinking is not operating like a damaged tool but is used incorrectly, due to changes in the broader aspects of personality organization. The language being used reveals the faulty abstraction since words become "individual," implying singular, fitting only specific objects or situations, and become, as it were, "part of the object." This observation encourages the assumption that schizophrenia is fundamentally a brain disorder, inasmuch as patients with organic brain damage show similar abnormalities in language.[7]

Investigators of this disorder find thinking to be not only concrete but literal, manifesting a difficulty with symbols or abstractions and a predilection for unusual symbolism and pseudoabstract thinking.[8] It is said that some thoughts occur that are mistakenly considered to be expressions of symbolic, metaphoric thinking. The term *symbols* in these statements signifies the verbal constituents of language, not mythic images: "Symbolic thinking belongs to higher forms of thinking which are equally impaired in schizophrenia."[9] When it is concluded that symbol formation is impaired and inappropriate, the statement is intended to imply that the language used, that is, to symbolize in terms of words, is not operating according to the rules of rational thought.

Yet in the view I am presenting a quite different species of symbols is at play in the acute episode, not belonging to the realm of rational functioning. Mythic symbols have in this condition supplanted the usual linguistic ones, and are being used to express images heavily laden with energy, thereby arresting the person's full attention. In the normative state these images tend to build up their own pyramiding hierarchies of structure towards a unitary whole, centered and balancing the opposites, finally embracing most of the vital issues of emotional living. There are, then, two hierarchic structures: the ego-conscious's rational system of concepts and feelings growing to ever higher levels of abstraction and unification; and the unconscious's nonrational system of meaning and values in ever deepening levels of imagery and unification. The higher and the deeper levels of symbols are counterparts of each other. Each creates its own experience of realness, its own different realities. The disadvantage of the nonrational systems is that they are not granted recognition and validation by our culture and viewed as representing a different reality, but only a defective one.

This model of the acute episode—in which the "fantasy" reveals forms that are not derived from outside but that express the contents of the deep psyche—offers a clear picture of a certain type of concretization different from that of the formal thought disorder of later stages. It concerns what is done with the ideation, rather than the form of its expression. There is no lack of abstraction, but it takes the shape of the mythic images from depth, rather than from the level of the rational mind's abstract concepts. The concretizing is found to consist of two persistent tendencies: one is to identify with the most favored of the mythic figures that make their appearance in the visionary process; the other is to project the unfavored ones out into the surrounding world. Instead of speaking of a vision or the felt presence of a divine personage, the individual *becomes* it; one *is* then the Second Coming of Christ *or is* the Virgin Mother or the Love Goddess. On the unfavored side, rather than recognizing the threat of an overturning of one's system of beliefs and values from within, one is the victim of enemy agents or of CIA sleuths lurking outside the window.

These two features, the tendency to identify and to project, are responsible for the impression of insanity in this process. This effect is most unfortunate for the fate of the acute process itself: when it is viewed as psychopathology it is thwarted from attaining its goals, while if it were more aptly recognized as spiritual in essence much damage could be averted. For instance, if the need to reconstruct one's world-image within becomes a mission to change the outer world, one of two eventualities can occur: if the person is highly gifted and charismatic he or she might be given a glowing reception as a leader of reforms; if not so endowed, he or she might be consigned to the degrading status of a disqualified outcast. When invalidated, one is seen as an invalid. A society that is religious—in the sense of living by its myth and attending to its demands—tends to value its visionaries and regard them as possessed by the spirit. A culture that is dedicated to secular and materialistic guidelines devalues such persons to the point of extrusion from the participation granted to "normal" people.

The concretization does not follow the lines of the formal thought disorder, but concerns instead the way of relating to the mythic images. These symbolic configurations are highly dynamic and can thus be very inflating. In our kind of culture it is healthier to take them on the symbolic level of understanding and apply them to one's inner life. If one is more than usually gifted, they might be accepted as having value for the culture, providing creative or spiritual contributions.

During my four decades of observing the acute first episode, I have been guided by the view that it is not a question of impairment or damage but rather a shift in energy. When a person finds herself in a state of acute distress, in circumstances that have assailed her most sensitive vulnerabilities, her psyche may be stirred into an imperative need to reorganize the Self. The deepest levels of the psychic organism are activated, and in consequence they draw vast amounts of energy to themselves and away from the higher levels. The whole field of awareness becomes flooded with archaic forms, the myth-styled images that are the natural contents of those deep levels. This condition represents not a flight from outer reality, as a device to retreat from unbearable fears, but a state of being overwhelmed by inner psychic events. The sense of reality shifts from outer to inner, and she finds herself immersed in a mythic world totally out of keeping with the consensual one. If circumstances are favorable at this point, the psyche may embark upon its reorganizational process in its own customary fashion (yet so *un*customary to our usual expectations).

In this framework, therefore, the higher functions are not seen as defective or impaired, but robbed of their energy. Even the physical organism is deprived of its usual level of performance: motivations to care for it drop away as nourishment and sleep are given less heed.

Remarkably, the behavior resembles the preparations for inducing altered states of consciousness by ritual fasting and sleep deprivation. The picture is of an almost brutal demand on the part of the deep psyche that all the reserves of the organism be commandeered to support its urgent processes. It is not that the entire organism is operating at a lower level of performance, but that one part only is functioning at such a high pitch of energy that all the other functions become deprived of it. Roland Fischer prefers the term "hyperphrenia" for this "high arousal state."[10]

The clinical or psychological symptomatology is then an expression of this state. The person is withdrawn in her " preoccupations" with "fantasy," which means her whole attention is absorbed in this spontaneous sequence of images. The affect is "dulled" or "inappropriate" until someone is willing to relate and respond to this inner experience. Investigators who put the person through tests are met with resistance, for there is no interest in such games when there are more urgent matters constantly making themselves felt inside, of which the investigator is quite oblivious. Hence an impression of "aloofness" is created;[11] this is ironic since to the person in this state it appears that the tester is the one who is aloof and unconcerned with the momentous things happening psychically.

A most impressive and valuable clinical experiment to measure the effects of invalidation has been conducted by Zarlock.[12] Twenty-five years ago he demonstrated the striking difference between the observable effects of medical and nonmedical regimens. The design was this: thirty men having a diagnosis of reactive schizophrenia and at least three months of hospitalization were observed under four different kinds of environmental conditions. Three of the milieux were nonmedical, being recreational, occupational, and social; a fourth was the medical model setting. Zarlock and other staff members would dress and act in ways appropriate to each environment. The verbal communications were all taped and evaluated in respect to pathological content and linguistic disorders, that is, to signs of thinking disorder. Records were kept of "rough approximations of time patients interacted or communicated with one another and the amount of time devoted to a particular activity." Patients were found to adopt "appropriate language, relevant content, and proper roles in different environments." They showed "an ability to behave according to the rules." Schizophrenic reactions were "almost entirely absent in non-medical settings and only a medical environment seems to have an efficacy to produce the characteristic symptomatology," since in that setting patients may conform to its tacit demands, in fulfilling which they "may become immersed in pathological language, content, and behavior."

The one-way communication between patient and therapist characteristic of medical environments effects an isolation or lack of communication among patients as a normal consequence. Zarlock concludes that "the evidence seems to support the assumption that language and role pathology are to some extent artifacts of a medical milieu"; if a person adopts the role of a patient he "may wish to fulfill the demands associated with that particular social position."

The prevailing psychiatric consensus now holds that the failing of the abstract attitude tends to progress malignantly if not put to a stop. This view leads to an injunction, on the part of most hospitals and teaching programs, not to encourage patient's dereistic, that is, nonrational talk, not to listen in a related way to these communications (or at least not beyond the first occasion when it is heard for diagnostic purposes). This policy is held out of the fear that to give too much attention to the nonrational would only support the tendency toward disorganization. Yet there is a contradiction in this line of psychiatric thinking:

It is observed that part of the person's plight is her isolation and social disarticulation. Her attempts at communication are viewed as failing because of the deficiency in the thought process, and in the consequent chagrin,[13] causing increasing degrees of withdrawal to mitigate the anxiety by an "escape from reality" and "retreat from reason."[14] Psychiatry attempts to counter this by urging the person to " socialize" and improve her "social skills," in contrast to her natural inclinations in this state. Heavy medication is administered to mend the thought disorder. This treatment regimen, to restore the socially disarticulated person to her social context, amounts to an all-out attack upon what nature is engaged in doing. She is to be made "normal" again, to help her back to the prepsychotic state; but the psyche is striving to dismantle that previous self in order to reorganize it along new lines.

Thus the person is caught between opposite pressures: one from the psyche to go through disorganization on the way to reorganization, and the other from the psychiatric system to put a stop to that and get back to "normal." Hence a whole new disarticulation is set up by the profession in that the staff will not relate to the person in a way that she would feel them to be connecting with her depth. Thus, if the profession insists upon a nonlistening stance in relation to her inner concerns, the sense of isolation mounts, as does her feeling of disqualification and invalidation by a harsh diagnostic label. All this can only thrust her more into the direction of the very madness and insanity that the treatment is intended to remedy.

We therefore have to ask a hard question. If the signs of "thought disorder" are at a minimum in the first acute episode and most pronounced in the chronic states, what is it that causes the worsening? Is it due to an insidious disease process that becomes relentlessly aggravated with the passage of time? Or is it that the "patient" feels isolated because the communications that she would prefer to express are blocked by psychiatric policy? I prefer to conclude the latter on two counts: one is that rage is mounting when this blocking happens, and the rage is devastating to the psyche. On the other count, when therapy allows full expression of these innermost concerns of the person, the rage subsides and the disorder clears up rapidly. If this is the case, we owe it to the person to cease trying to correct her behavior and speech and instead to correct our own reception of her concerns. Such a new appraisal of the effects of the psyche's energy shift requires that we open ourselves to the various dimensions of visionary experience in the following discussion.

Chapter 3

Psychosis or Visionary State?

Having reviewed the psychiatric viewpoints and formulations of acute psychosis, we must look with new eyes at what it shows itself to be in its own nature as visionary experience of various sorts. While I learned much from each of my various clinical experiences, Diabasis provided the most unexpected revelations of what an acute episode can become when it is handled in this particular manner. Our criteria for admission to our facility were that it should be geared primarily for first acute episodes (of what is now defined as "brief psychotic disorder" or "schizophreniform disorder"); if not the first, then the episode should at least consist of an intense activation of the "deep" psyche, that is, one productive of rich myth-styled ideation and process. We accepted only those clients who gave indications of their intent really to work with their psyche.

Despite the usual assumption and teaching, we found that in the midst of an acute episode psychotherapy in depth can be very fruitful. Such therapy seemed the most natural course to take since the most urgent issues and conflicts are out in the open at such a time; the basic injuries and hurts of early childhood are being reexperienced, ready to be worked on with considerable intensity. What made this therapeutic work possible was the unexpected occurrence that we found, as already mentioned, of our clients' coming out of their fragmented state into clarity and coherency within a few days after admission more frequently than not. This turn for the better was due primarily to the manner of our acceptance of them and the fact that their inner concerns and ideation were given respect, interest, and affirmation from the start. Episodes characterized by the richest outpouring of imagery, while appearing the most disturbed, were the most favorable for good outcomes.

Of course, in psychiatric circles, to pay attention to the mental content, with its "bizarre ideation" in "psychosis," is frowned upon and even regarded as fruitless; in many hospitals this is even forbidden because it is seen as harmful. I have never been in agreement with this dismissal. Once we relate to the person's inner experience with a caring acceptance and interest, the ideation may cease to remain an assortment of strange ideas in a state of fragmentation. Instead, an inner process may soon be revealed which turns out to be entirely meaningful and about which we have much to learn.

A young woman came to the county hospital with the belief that she was a witch and had the evil eye; she thought she was being punished for this and wanted to be baptized; also that she had died and was in an afterlife state. She had visions of the time of the creation and of early evolution, and of the first primitive peoples migrating across the continents. Her mind took her back to scenes of her childhood. She was frightened at being caught up in a struggle between the two great world powers, Communism and Democracy, with her at the center of plots and counterplots, each trying to make use of her knowledge, even poisoning her. All the feminine women were to be sent away. While watching a lightning storm, she had visions of a series of great holy men—Moses, Paul, and Luther—and in great exultation received the revelation that she was to be the fourth and a leader of a new religious era. Each was the reincarnation of the same great divine spirit. There were allusions to her being the new Virgin Mother and Queen but this was to be kept secret. The Bay Area was a world center about to become a new hell while a new Heavenly City, a New Bethlehem, was to drop from the sky in spaceships, bringing a whole new order into the world as an achievement of science. This would be the New Jerusalem placed at the center of the world. There was to be no single new savior but every eldest son was to be a Son of Man, all perfect men knowing everything of importance for the world's welfare. People would then have the wisdom to enable them to live sensibly together in peace.

Now while all this play of images appears much too grandiose and far from reason, all that is required is to transpose them from their projection into the world of outer events, to a recognition of them as events in her inner psychic life. In this way we find in them an entirely meaningful portrayal of processes within her psyche. I have, of course, omitted many other features of her process and of her early and recent relationships, in order to bring a few significant points into high relief.

In an acute psychosis individuals undergo a profound reorganization of the self, effected by a thoroughgoing reintegration through utter disintegration. (Dabrowski,[1] who taught at Johns Hopkins, expounded on this theme at length.) Even more than this, these persons experience a basic refurbishing of their inner, subjective culture in terms of the images of society and of the world itself. The world-image and self-image are alike and are represented in the same symbolic expression by a quadripartite circular design; and the flow of associations portrays specific cultural ideologies pertaining to each quadrant of this image. In this manner the reforming of the self becomes equivalent to the reforming of one's worldview. Much of the work done by the psychotic process concerns a dissolution of the self-image and its renewal in parallel with a destruction of the world-image and its ensuing regeneration. These concerns and others can be worked with very effectively in psychotherapy, even in the very midst of the acute "psychotic" state.

Working with the psyche in the mode under discussion, there is a great advantage in letting the process run its course freely in psychotherapy without its suppression by medication. In this framework the images are regarded as representing emotions and emotional issues. Jung has formulated these myth-styled configurations as archetypes, manifesting in image and emotion,[2] which belong together. I therefore have suggested the term *affect-image* to make the concept a bit less formidable. We know that medications suppress these components of the psyche, particularly the emotion, an intent that to me seems ironic since the dulling of the affect is the major problem in this state. Our experimental projects have indicated that going through the whole experience without medication allows the image process to proceed and the emotions to mature in consequence.

Our outcome studies tell the tale. The three-year follow-up on eighty-one cases in the Agnew Project[3] showed 73% recurrence of the psychosis in patients treated with medication both in and out of the hospital, but only 8% of those treated without medication both in and out. The personality profiles were even more striking: those on medication showed arrest in emotional development over the three years of the follow-up, while those off medication showed no such plateauing of the growth curve, but a continuous upward rise. The reports of these findings have been ignored almost totally, perhaps because this kind of news in unwelcome and inconvenient.

I have found a regularly recurring sequence of images in case after case. This observation led me to investigate an extensive array of myth-and-ritual forms that parallel this particular pattern; these are the renewal rites of the earliest city cultures of the ancient world.[4] Looking further I encountered other situations in which this renewal process made its appearance, namely in the visionary experience of prophets and reformers.[5] In the fields of cultural anthropology and psychological anthropology a considerable literature has developed since World War II, manifesting our new encounter with the phenomena of acculturation and rapid culture change, in which prophets figure prominently.

I will cite a couple of instances of such visionary leaders. The first was the story, in nineteenth century China, of the visions of Hung,[6] who led the powerful T'ai-P'ing rebellion and almost succeeded in winning the "Mandate of Heaven" to inaugurate a new dynasty. When a young man, he failed the imperial examinations for a political post and, in the shock of this humiliation, fell into a stupor of six weeks' duration. While his family thought him to be dying, he was in fact suffering over-whelming visions of traveling out into the realm of Heaven, where the deceased ancestors dwell, and receiving instructions there from their chief to reform the kingdom and usher in a new age. He returned from these visions with a new sturdiness of character and a strong charisma, now equipped for political leadership. He gathered a large following and an army so that he was able to govern all of southern China from Nanking as his capital; he later almost was able to overthrow the dynasty and rule as Son of Heaven, but was opposed by the Western powers.

The second instance was the story of the Seneca tribe of Native Americans, which had become a dispirited slum culture under the new white dominance. Handsome Lake[7] was an inconspicuous member who fell into a state of profound shame after breaking some taboos while drunk. He became ill and was thought to be dying, but in his stupor traveled out into the regions of heaven, where he perceived, among other things, that the world was being threatened with imminent destruction by a "Great Sickness" brought upon it by a bright colored light, in the shape of a huge drop hanging in the sky. He was taught by spirits how to avert this fate through the agency of an opposite drop of light and of a reformation of his people by a new set of laws and rituals. Under his leadership, after his recovery, his nation became rehabilitated and revitalized into a strong community with high morale.

Lanternari[8] lists headings of a composite account of prophetic experiences:

> There is a return to the conditions of the society's beginnings in the Golden Age. The dead rise and return. A cataclysm is a prelude to the end of the world. A struggle against foreign influence and power is launched and reversal of the social order results. The world is regenerated and [a] new Golden age is inaugurated. The messiah who recreates the world and restores the tradition is the new personification of the long-awaited ancestral culture hero who first founded the society and its lineage of leadership.

These experiences not only indicate a similarity to the "psychotic" visionary states I am describing, but even seem to be composed of the same psychological process, and thus to be similar not only in appear-ance but in kind, not only analogous but homologous.

What, then, distinguishes the "psychotic" experience from the visionary? The prophet has, of course, an above-average intelligence and a fund of information with which to process and assimilate his visions, but also he is endowed with a creative capacity and a contagious charisma by which he can influence his culture profoundly. For this effect, however, the nature of his visions must be such that they become accepted by the society. The reception of his visions seems to depend on their correspondence with the psychic concerns of the populace, which provide a readiness within the minds of the people to hear this particular new myth form as voiced by the prophet.

The "patient" in a visionary experience also may be intelligent, well informed, and creative, but he or she may have a more urgently important task of another kind. This is the requirement of his or her own inner development, not letting the aim rest at the level of social protest, however much that might occur. The affective forcefulness, the impact on the listener, and the persuasiveness are altogether different than the prophet's. To safeguard this inner work of personal development, it is necessary to provide a secure, favorable, and private haven, apart from the confusion engendered in the ordinary environment by people's reactions to unusual states of consciousness.

The prophet's visions are intended to heal the society; the "patients" are to heal the self, regardless of whatever might occur afterwards from any creative work emanating from them.

The suggestion I propose, then, is that in cases of acute episode of visionary experience we must be open to any of several possibilities:

1. The persons might be capable of leadership in religion, social reform, or the arts or sciences and their potential contribution to society is making its first appearance in a "psychotic" turmoil, the rich potentials of which are being seen at first only as expressions of symbolic imagery.

2. The persons might be caught up in an inner process of self-reorganization, activated with the intent of releasing hidden potentials for living an increasingly fruitful life of caring relationships and creative work.

3. The persons might be in the throes of a disintegrative process that will lead gradually into the downhill course and chronicity of true "schizophrenia" after six months.

These alternatives deserve quite different handling from the start, ideally, if we could but devise a set of criteria to judge their differential diagnosis directly The first group needs to be left alone by psychiatry and consigned to other forms of retreat where the visions can be tolerated, accepted, and appreciated for their actual value, and thus allowed to do their own work in nature's way. The second group needs to be handled sensitively without the negative impact of "labelling,"[9] and without their identifying with the status of "patienthood"[10] in a hospital setting, but rather with a stay in a nonhospital setting where the psychic process can be encouraged by an openly receptive attitude to the inner process and where medication would be unnecessary or held at bare minimum. The third group, because of the impoverished state of our knowledge at present, needs medication early to prevent damage to brain functioning and undue chronicity, as well as early referral to a half way-house or board-and-care housing.

Since the persons in all three categories can appear quite "insane" at the start, we may envision a homelike facility for observation of any new admissions in these states for a few days, providing of course that there are favorable indications in regard to the previous history of the client, their personality, and their intelligence. By that time it should be possible to assess to which group each belongs.

How, then, can we identify at the time of admission, which of these alternative eventualities a new applicant is going to be capable of? Our present accumulation of general clinical observations and the resulting data do not provide relevant material with which to evaluate the likelihood of a favorable future course of the episode, since these records show assessments that are the product of many factors that have influenced the "patient's" inner process. The very fact that we label, medicate, and hospitalize almost universally and automatically closes off all possibilities of learning new things about the inner psychic functions and processes involved, and therefore about favorable modes of handling them. Fear governs much of our policy-making in this regard, leading us to avoid attempting anything so "high-risk" as allowing the visionary states to continue. With the familiar occurrence of damage from heavy medications, it can just as well be said that this way is even more risky than seeing a person through the episode without such interventions.

There is much to be learned about the psychic turmoil that, with our present procedures, we prevent ourselves from recognizing. We urgently need new approaches that might provide us the opportunity to observe, and thus to distinguish among the diagnostic variables those that are crucial for identifying which persons may be expected to have favorable inner experiences and which modes of therapy may be best for facilitating them.

Chapter 4

Alternative Ways

In view of all that has just been said, we turn our attention now from the psychiatric standpoint to the more practical issue of the place of psychotherapy in the handling of the acute episodes where the inner process is given its proper valuation and respect. Because the decade of the 1980s has seen the almost universal consensus mentioned earlier, that so-called schizophrenia is a brain disorder and that its treatment relies altogether upon medication, psychotherapy for the acute episodes is given little heed, time, or funding. Indeed in most facilities it is even forbidden for staff members to talk with clients about their inner experience, ideation, or emotions because it might have the effect of increasing the extent of the disorder. Keeping the hospital ward's atmosphere quiet and undisturbed occupies the attention of the staff more than the needs of individuals for self-expression

In contrast to these prevailing conventions, alternatives to hospitalization have been attempting in residence facilities to provide a more humane atmosphere, with attitudes that are nonauthoritarian, nonlabeling, and nonobjectifying, and with ample time given to relating to their clients. Consequent favorable effects have been tabulated in Mosher's reports.[1]

The virtues of these alternative ways speak for themselves, but there are deeper reasons for preferring them that come to light if we dare to sit down and spend time just being with a client. We have noted that as we shift our concern from symptomatology and pathology to the actual content of the person's experience, quite unexpected things begin to happen and the "clinical" picture changes rapidly. I am speaking of the acute and preferably the first episode.

The other way, when the episode is handled in the manner that is customary today, if we show that the flow of thought and imagery draws a blank and that we regard it as "bizarre" and of no worth, the patient withdraws further and "clams up." Then the doors of communication are slammed shut and the individual assumes the guise and identity of "patient" instead of remaining a person in a valid emotional crisis. He or she might agree to become a "good" patient in behavior, with the practical aim of an early discharge, but more likely would become sullenly resistive or filled with rage.

If we do sit quietly with a client and spend time with ease, giving lively responses that express our recognition of the meaningfulness of what is being communicated, then surprising results follow. The general fragmentation changes very soon to a clear coherency and an urge to reveal; even more importantly, the content of the ideation begins to assume a certain direction and sense of purpose or aim. The first quarter-hour usually determines how the episode is going to go, whether toward fragmentation or towards coherency We will be tested for a time, to see whether we really are willing to be open-minded listeners, but once that has been tried out and passed, an intense relation is set up in which good work can be accomplished.

At Diabasis, I participated in an intake session with another staff member, admitting a young woman whom we accepted from a county hospital. There her hostile behavior had proved so unmanageable that she was about to be sent to the state hospital, with a prediction of a stay of several months. She arrived in a straightjacket and in the company of two helmeted men in white, each one holding an arm. She was still mute, as she had been on the ward. We unburdened her of the straight-jacket and spent a couple of hours of nonverbal exchange with her, in which she pulled us close and threw us back several times. When she indicated thirst and we brought her a fruit juice, she threw it in our faces; to this we said quietly that she had a right to express angry feelings but we did not appreciate this way of conveying it. She went to bed and fell into a sound sleep for twelve hours. When she awoke the next morning, she became talkative and perfectly coherent, as well as docile. She refused therapeutic sessions until, after a few weeks, she developed fond feelings toward a male staff member and painted a portrait of him; her transference bore good fruit over the ensuing weeks in therapy.

Another young woman at Diabasis arrived in a mute state, deeply withdrawn. However, she gave indications of her wish to be held and cuddled. When a couple of staff persons received her in their arms and enfolded her in a warm blanket, her cheeks began to show the cus-tomary suckling movements. In response a baby bottle with warm milk was offered and imbibed with relish. After another day of these exchanges she awoke in the morning full of talk and readiness to relate coherently, and she soon was dancing to rock music with delightful verve.

It is all too easy to assume that a client in an initial resistive with-drawal does not want either that we relate to her or that she relate to us.

It turns out, though, despite such appearances, that persons in this kind of episode want desperately to be heard and understood, and are highly appreciative when they are. To be listened to with respect and understanding seems to have an effect like entering a magical space—hence the quick changes I have just sketched.

So what is so wonderful about being heard? one might ask.

When in the "high arousal state," the sense of reality having shifted from the customary, consensual outer world to the inner world of mythic cast, of cosmic beings and sacred events, the individual is perceived to be withdrawn. The fact of the matter is that it is we of the outer world who usually do the withdrawing to avoid having to come too close to the eeriness of that unfamiliar, nonrational psychic atmosphere. Hence the client's withdrawal is the natural result of expecting not to be heard and understood by others. The gulf between is a mutual creation and disaster.

Yet if and when we do listen with respectful attentiveness and lively responsiveness, not only is the abyss of separation bridged but a sequence of imagery begins to unfold. As the relationship becomes increasingly secure and warm, a somewhat orderly process emerges from the disorder of fragmented forms. Usually the client feels increasingly enthusiastic about what is occurring and opens up with a flow of concerns, most of which are apt to be of a symbolic nature.

At the start impressions are conveyed of having been in the throes of dying and being in the afterlife, or of being at some world Center and back at the time of creation and simultaneously at the time of one's own beginnings in infancy or childhood. Now a whole inner journey is under way that has a very complex itinerary, and we find ourselves in for a shared adventure in a mythic space, as if an entire myth and ritual procedure were waiting to reveal itself step by step. Often it seems the client can hardly wait till the next session to tell the progress of events in this inner drama.

The image sequence occurs with some regularity from case to case, as in the instance of the young lady recounted in the last chapter.[2] After establishing a center and undergoing the death and return to the beginnings, there follows a cosmic conflict of opposing values or forces, a threat of the opposite sex, a grandiose apotheosis, a sacred marriage, a new birth, and a messianic program for a new society or culture; throughout these motifs there prevails a mandala-shaped, quadripartite world-image as their frame. To recognize the significance of these themes, it helps to realize that they follow closely the same pattern as that of the ancient myth and ritual of renewal in the sacral kingships that make their appearance with the rise of the city cultures in the urban revolution leading to the Bronze Age. This renewal process is vivid and dramatic, commanding the full attention of the person in this state, and should not be stifled by medication.

It has been observed and reported by researchers for half a century and more that spontaneous recoveries occur. Outstanding among these was Anton Boisen,[3] who in the 1920s did extensive researches on a large number of cases at Worcester State Hospital, noting in their imagery several of the motifs just outlined. Boisen found that at least 10 percent of cases recovered spontaneously. Some remissions have been reported by more recent investigators as reaching higher proportions, as much as 30 percent.[4] If it were possible to select those who are in the renewal process, my belief is that the number of recoveries would climb to at least 70 percent. Our Agnew Project did at least demonstrate the superiority of the regimen without medication but with placebo, by which all but 8 percent showed no recurrence in the three-year follow-up.[5]

Our results were different from some other research experiments investigating the same question, several of which showed poor outcomes in the nonmedicated cases. However, Gunderson,[6] in reviewing these contradictory conclusions, found the relevant factor to be the attitudes toward psychosis and its treatment on the part of the staff: favorable outcomes without medication varied together with the more accepting and relating ways, as in our project, while negative ones varied together with the more conventional authoritarian and judgmental views accompanied by law-and-order policies.

Diabasis did not take the stand of being a totally medication-free facility out of principle. The intent at its founding was to offer help to persons through their first acute episode without medication; our financing was assured, leaving us free to hold to our model (with two exceptions). After losing in an unfortunate contention with other services competing for money, ending in our closure, we recovered from a two-year demise as Diabasis II. This time support was not assured and necessity demanded that we veer from our model by taking other kinds of cases to such an extent that only one fifth of our admissions conformed to it. We learned from this circumstance that the program works best if the atmosphere of the facility is kept strictly clean of any implication of sickness.

It is clear that clients prefer a regimen in which the staff work by these humane qualities of warmth and acceptance.[7] Yet it is not enough to conclude merely that power, controllingness, authoritarian modes, and pyramidal hierarchies are not good and that democratic regimes and horizontal structures are good, and thus account for better effects. A more precise reason for preferring these alternative ways concerns the nature of the process being experienced in the psyche and of the response to it. The renewal of the self and of its cultural preferences is the core issue, involving one's sense of identity and way of being in the world, that is, the accompanying worldview. Now coming to one's self, discovering who one is, is not a cognitive matter and is not a task to be accomplished alone. Rather, it requires mutual feeling in a caring relationship with warm affirmation. There seems to be something about this kind of relatedness that troubles psychiatric staffs enough to keep it out of discussion. It is outlandish enough to suggest that a therapist in this work should be ready for dialogue over myth and ritual imagery (that is, over religious and spiritual concerns). Now even more unbecoming would be this suggestion: only if there is an atmosphere of loving caring and affirmation running through the entire facility can this process reach its proper ends. The reason for such a suggestion is that a person's new selfhood comes into being within the containment of a devoted relationship in which an enthusiastic reception of the renewed self is overt.

In our American culture we cannot boast of having accomplished much differentiated consciousness in matters of loving relationships. In consequence there is every chance that an intent to be loving, in the sense under discussion, might be misguided and manifested only in sentimental expressions of pseudo-feelings of good will. A truly caring reception of a client just emerging into a true selfhood entails open and genuinely revealing responses made of real emotions and feelings. Staff members cannot expect unguarded expressions from a client unless they are willing to be open as well, as models of the way to be natural in one's interchanges. This creates a pervasive atmosphere of emotional realness and truth.

To sum up briefly the nature of therapy with the renewal process, the acute episode is found classically to last some six weeks, the oft-mentioned forty days. In it the Self is undergoing a transformative series of processes while held in a containing transference relationship with one or two staff persons. One speaks with the client without any note of condescension, without any implication of the presence of abnormality or sickness, but rather in the spirit of communicating directly with the healthy normative ego as if it were present and intact in the client's psyche, even when made invisible by the turmoil of the initial fragmentation. As the renewal process gets under way, the new self needs to be sensitively given perceptive recognition and encouragement. This kind of caring response with affirmation is the same as Rogers's "unconditional positive regard."[8] A genuinely loving response is a frank and honest one, conveying what one sees and how one feels in reaction to whatever comes up. In no way does it call for a sweet or false kindly stance. The intent is, on the contrary, to establish an actual community of persons, of staff and clients alike, who are genuinely caring in their relations with one another and openly expressive.

Psychotherapy of a very effective and penetrating kind under these circumstances becomes not only possible but even the natural course of events. Psychiatric textbooks make the opposite statement, that psychotherapy is quite out of the question during the period of the "psychosis" and must wait for at least a year for more favorable conditions. Such dire conclusions as these are based on the assumption that the progress of development and integration is the work of the ego, through the conscious insight gained from interpretive formulation. The point of view I am speaking for is that in the acute episode the autonomous psyche is doing the essential work and moves at a fast pace into issues that need attention. The pace seems to be proportional to the intensity of the "disturbance," that is, to the degree of the psyche's activation in its high arousal state.

This autonomy of the psyche in providing the lead in the process is, as I see it, the real justification for having, for this kind of therapeutic work, a staff of paraprofessionals without extensive psychological education and training. These beginning staff members learn on the job, like apprentices, with regular consultations and conferences to facilitate their understanding. They are selected on the basis of their comfort with unusual states of consciousness, their unintrusive allowingness, and their capacity for caring.

Another significant justification for the role of the staff is that coming newly into this work, they can be comfortably receptive to the strange states of consciousness and processes without the prejudices and negative expectations that a thorough education in psychopathology and diagnostic labeling creates. This kind of therapy is different from that used with the chronic psychotic conditions; in those the psyche is not in the high arousal state and hence does not do the work that is done in the acute conditions, unless intensive therapy induces activation through the transference, as seen, for instance, in an account of an impressive case by Dr. Howard Levene:[9] A young married woman was in the familiar plight of chronicity of so-called schizophrenia, being seen in the outpatient service twice monthly for checking on her medications. When he decided she might do better with weekly interviews in psychotherapy, things began to change. Her drawings expressing her feelings in her relations with him progressed from black-and-white stick figures to full-page displays of flowers in vivid, rich colors. She, of course, was at the same time coming to experience her emotions with warm vitality.

The question naturally springs to mind, does not this kind of therapy require knowledgeable and skillful interpretations? The myth-styled images and processes surely seem at first quite abstruse and far from ordinary experience, becoming a major factor in their dismissal from psychiatric consideration as "bizarre ideation." In my experience it has usually been found to be enough to recognize the meaningfulness of the images. The renewal process goes on of itself and does its work regardless of thorough understanding. It does, however, require an intensive relationship with a partner in the work, attended by mutual feeling that animates the process and helps it keep on track as it moves ahead phase by phase.

During the staff member's apprenticeship the images keep recurring again and again, in case after case, so that in time they become familiar; then a modicum of reading or instruction is found helpful and interesting, though perhaps not necessary. I have had to remind myself that a staff member's first exposure to the images is not unlike what I went through when first beginning to work with such clients, and that the learning process was the same for me. I like to view this recognition of the meaning of the images as "informed listening." With this reception doing its part, the client knows from day to day that the staff partner in the work is "with it." I often find that it seems to be enough even that the staff member's face lights up on hearing the mention of an image, or a move in the process, as if to say, "Yes, I know."

Then, beyond this recognition of the meaningfulness of the image is a further move on the therapist's part. With a certain client he or she has been hearing from day to day of many emotionally sensitive issues; when an image makes its appearance one may be able to perceive a link to one of these concerns, as its metaphorical expression. I like to call this linking simply "making connections,"[10] in place of offering complicated interpretations that always depend on an accompanying theoretic frame-work. When such a connection is on target there is a surprising effect on the client, evoking not only an "Aha!" response, but even better, often creating a significant leap ahead in progress.

In this regard, from the various splittings of the psyche's functions observed by Bleuler[11] (with fragmentation of associations, of the line of thought, and of the affects), one stands out here. What makes the acute first episode "psychotic" rather than purely visionary is the already mentioned splitting of the affect from the ideation, creating a state of mind in which there is a veritable cascade of images filling the field of awareness, but in which these have lost their emotional concomitants. Making connections between the symbolic image and the personal emotional context in which it arises thus has a healing effect by restoring the emotion to the image.

In discussions of this mode of therapy the question "Where does family therapy fit in?" is naturally raised. In answer the overall picture of the tasks to be accomplished can be divided into two main phases, that of interior work and then that of repairing one's relation to the outer setting. At no point can it be overlooked that troubles have been engendered in the family system, in that "psychosis" has become an essential component of that system with the client as the "identified patient,"[12] in the majority of cases. The pathologizing and labelling[13] that usually starts in the family setting is then repeated in the psychiatric one, which ironically enough frequently reenacts the familial pattern with uncanny exactness.

The phase of inner work is the all-engrossing renewal process, which, in the light of the family system, has as its aim the death of the faulty self-image engendered in that early web of unconscious interrelations between parents and siblings. There follows the regeneration of the self-image, which then needs to be protected and encouraged in the new setting of persons who can greet it with real nurturance and provide a favorable soil in which to grow. Along with this, the world-image representing the subculture established in the family now also undergoes dissolution followed by regeneration, which also needs safeguarding. For this purpose, the lifestyle, value system, and belief system of the staff play a vitally important role in providing a safe space for the client's new personal, subjective culture-form to emerge and become established.

The early phase of the acute episode requires withdrawal from the ordinary environment and its accustomed relationships in order to permit a requisite freedom for new things to happen. Frequently it is observed that some encounters with the family during this time can have devastating effects upon this very sensitive process. For a helpful comparison we need only be reminded of rites of passage in tribal societies:[14] in these ceremonies the child being initiated is isolated from family and community for a period of time until he is ready to return, newly born and ready for adulthood, never to live within the family circle again.

Only after the experience of the first few weeks and in the second phase, with a still fragile sense of new identity and outlook, is the client ready to deal with the family, and only after recognizing in the midst of the psychic turmoil what has gone wrong in the early parental relationships. At this point there is a need to confront the family and work through the strong emotions of pain and hurt; the effort is to establish a new independence and capacity to defend oneself in the face of noxious emotional tangles. During the vulnerable period of the early weeks of the episode, the client has been dealing with the parental figures inwardly and has gone through changes in relation to them, but the parents usually have not, and in consequence a modicum of self-assurance is needed for the client to cope with the family.

I must reiterate that the model of the episode and its therapy that I am describing is appropriate to the acute form only, and preferably the first acute episode. Acuteness in this sense is identified by the intense activation of the deep psyche in its "high arousal state,"[15] made recognizable by a lively outpouring of imagery that shows itself to be of great concern to the client. Chronic states, on the other hand, require a different regimen and should not be included here.

For the most fruitful handling of this kind of acute episode a residence with a homelike setting is vastly preferable, as little suggestive of a hospital or clinic as possible. In it the aim is to keep the atmosphere clear of any implications of sickness. The difficulty with mixing a population of chronic cases in their third or fourth "decompensation" is that they are usually in a more or less demoralized state with low energy, having conformed to the picture of "patienthood" that the psychiatric regimen has inculcated.[16] This striking picture of sickness conveys a discouraging impression of what might lie ahead for the person newly arrived in a first episode; this failure of the renewal process to do its natural work is precisely what the residence facility attempts to avoid by declining to thwart it. When the client community is composed of persons in the high arousal state there prevails a buoyant, lively, eager, and warm feeling tone with a lot of horseplay, fun, and dancing, as well as creative work and intense conversations in relationships that become quite affectionate.

To preserve the spirit in which the episode could be most fruitfully handled, at Diabasis a message was clearly spoken to each new client upon admission to the community: "This is not a disease, illness, or psychopathology. It is a rich inner experience in a visionary state that may be turbulent and scary at times, sometimes nightmarish and sometimes sublime, yet that's all tending to move toward a goal that is favorable for a better life. We're here to help you with it." With this counsel the clients could fit into a forward-looking expectation fully as much as in hospitals they would fit into the very negative expectation of the conventional psychiatric model of a meaningless disorder and consequent crippling handicap.

Our aim at Diabasis was to lift these individuals out of the Mental Health System's flowchart, with its design of a long career beginning at a crowded crisis-unit, leading to a community mental health ward or a "locked facility," thence to a half-way house and ending at a board-and-care home with biweekly visits to an outpatient clinic. That entire program is very expensive and also stifling to nature's healing process. The characteristic outcome for persons undergoing the renewal process in our residence was that at the time of discharge they were ready for new moves in their lives and for meeting them with fullness of energy.

In order to understand this readiness for a fuller life after the episode, we need to look into the entire context of the renewal process both in the smaller subculture of the facility and also in the broader culture viewed in its historical perspective.

Chapter 5

Transitions in Outlook

It usually is of some advantage in psychological discussions to start with vivid impressions of what actually happens with persons in their human plights and how they experience them; then we can move on from there into questions of what we may make of them—quite a secondary matter. The experience itself is always at the heart of anything of value said about "psychotic" episodes, and is the most reliable.

Let me sketch out the scene at Diabasis as if it were here in the present even though in actuality it has been closed since the late 1970s.

It is a home, a three-family apartment house converted into one household, in downtown San Francisco. Walking in you find a sitting room, dining room, and kitchen open to one another. It is evening; there is a fire going in the sitting room with some persons gathered there for a poetry reading. Others are clustered around the dining table in lively conversation, and a few others are cooking something in the kitchen. As you look around, you cannot tell who is staff and who is client. The atmosphere is of a warm feeling and usually is quiet and mellow. There might be some disturbance downstairs in what is called the rage room, occasioning the awkward circumstance that we find ourselves with a "padded cell"! It is not a "seclusion room" but a safe space to let go with anger and convey it to a staff person. This is the setting, with an atmosphere that is more than friendly—it is affectionate. This entire house is a place where clients can feel comfortable about expressing any kind of concern and trust that what they speak about will be respected and found meaningful.

When one does listen to these contents—this ideation that is so far away and so mythological—it seems sometimes so disconnected from everyday life that one asks oneself, "Well, so why listen to all of that?" This is the customary attitude in psychiatry: "Why listen to it all? It has nothing to do with present problems, or parents." Instead of talking about Mom and Dad, it may be objected, they are talking about the Sky Father and Earth Mother, and how does one get to anything significant that way? How do we credit the flow of talk at all?

This type of ideation in the acute episode tends to fly off in all directions. There are many cultural implications, mythical ones, even elements of mystical states or sociopolitical ideologies. I will try to sketch out briefly one particular aspect that I consider to be the major thrust of the process: the transition in outlook or worldview.

A young man, about thirty, came in for admission with a story that he had had a vision. In it he saw coming into the bay a flotilla of ships carrying Zen Buddhists. It was a kind of migration of a new culture into the Bay Area to bring a transformation of California's. He rushed out to greet these invaders because he felt he was supposed to have a part in the new change. Of course, in his disturbed state he was noticed by someone who called the police, and thus he was brought in.

He was a very successful young businessman in electronics, living in suburbia with his wife and children, energetic and masterful in his trade. This new concern about Buddhism did not seem to belong to that whole pattern of his life; it was even alien to it. After a few days with us he developed a way of pulling at the fire alarm and setting off its loud bell many times a day. The clanging din stirred such a commotion time and again that it became intensely irritating to the staff to the degree that they were not sure they could keep him in our program. Somehow everyone weathered it, though, even with gongs filling the air every twenty minutes. Only after all this action was it revealed that he was acting in accord with further visions, in which he was witnessing the world dissolving away in flames and hellish things happening within this all-consuming fire. The world was burning up, and he himself would soon go up in flames. In this way the themes of death and world-destruction were coinciding. Soon there followed visions of the void before the creation of the cosmos, beautiful ones in which little points of light like jewels became circles and chains and finally organized themselves into new galaxies. Thus was born a whole refurbished world-image.

By the end of the first week or ten days, we were quite aware that this man was absolutely riven between two alternative ways of living: he was on the one hand not quite daring to drop out of the conservative, suburban life he had been living up to this point, but on the other, a new mystical potential was developing in him that was becoming more and more demanding of his attention. This new possibility was capturing his energies and captivating his imagination. He was having thoughts of attending the Zen Center or another Buddhist program of instruction, perhaps retiring for a year or two there. These quests offered lifestyles for him quite different from that of his home and business, and he found himself suspended in the middle between them. He left us at the end of his two months not knowing which way to decide his course, and we gave no advice on which choice might be best, leaving it up to him to work that out.

In staff conferences we often found ourselves saying of such and such a client and her imagery, as we discussed her progress in her experience, that it sounded very much like a culture change that this person was undergoing. A staff member would exclaim, "Yes! That is what she is saying to us—that she's aware of going through a cultural change and a transition into something new." I am left with the conviction that changes on this level constitute the keynote of what is transpiring in the visionary process of the acute episode. I will attempt to explicate just how, as I envision it, that shift comes about and what it seems to imply about how such transformation is effected, and about what it is in the psyche that drives the process.

Diabasis was founded on the premise that the psyche knows what it is intending. Our staff members were not all particularly Jungian in persuasion and did not belong to any one school of thought. Yet we all agreed on the point that the psyche was up to its own devices and that we would do well to give heed to its expressions and encourage them, respond to them and help them do their work. The best one can do is to follow the lead that the psyche provides. The unconventional aspect of this view is that with cases of extremely disturbed and confused states of mind, it is still true that the psyche's way can be trusted to reveal its own modes of achieving its own ends, that is, by its myth-making process.

For most psychiatrists the difficulty is that the psyche's way of expressing itself is so unusual that we find ourselves having to speak in an entirely unaccustomed language and frame of thought. In the alternative view, the concept of the acute "psychosis" is that, when we speak of a self-healing process, we do not mean that the faults to be healed are these unusual expressions of the devices the psyche uses to attain its goals. Instead, the problems needing solution are in the limitations of the personality prevailing before the episode; the psyche is trying to break free from constrictions, from a markedly negative self-image, a rather impoverished world outlook, and an unsuitable cultural set. The upheaval takes place in those persons whose nature cannot tolerate such limitations. The visionary devices set in motion by the psyche therefore do not constitute the disorder or pathology. In the turmoil the psyche's process is not what needs healing, but rather, the healing is accomplished by the "psychotic" process itself. The way we regard the disturbance, they, determines how it is going to fare, whether toward success or failure.

The "healing power of nature," which used to be called the *vis mediatrix naturae*, is of the essence when we are considering the question of a self-organizing process. The best medicine in medieval times, deriving from more ancient eras, followed the way of nature to move through a disease process; one did not oppose the disease process but worked with the organism's endowments. In our age of mastery and technology, we tend to forget this philosophy and to take control and authority into medical hands with the techniques of medical science. In the way alternative approaches are advocating now, we are obliged to assume a more humble stance and relate to the remedial ways of nature, not allowing ourselves to feel that they must be overcome or driven out.

For five years I worked with acute episodes, hearing the dramatic experiences of death and birth, creation and destruction, and societal programs of reform, without comprehending why ideologies of politics and government took such a prominent place. Only when I read Mircea Eliade's *The Myth of the Eternal Return*[1] did I finally recognize why the images assumed this particular configuration. The sequence belonged to the myths and rituals of ancient city kingdoms of the Bronze Age, the first truly urban cultures. I will briefly point out what was important about that history for our understanding of visionary states today.

At the beginning of city culture there was a tremendously profound transformation of the structure of society involving ethics, morals, and design of life. Visionaries established new mythic systems at that turning point: they projected the image of the world Center onto the royal figure governing the society, as will be seen in chapter 10.[2] This sacral king's ceremonial function was to undergo, in ritual practice, the very procedures that in our time we recognize as interior psychic process: the annual New Year festival[3] represented the renewal of king and kingdom in a drama that followed a sequence identical to that which we see in the visionary states of persons in the acute episode. The locus of this procedure was designated as the world Center or cosmic axis around which the kingdom extended into a mandala shape, at least ideally, thus expressing a concretization and actualization of the image. The regal figure at the Center carried the image representing symbolically the "Unique Man," the only one capable of rebirth, immortality, or transformation.

The "urban revolution"[4] became also in time an age of extreme violence, when there came into being for the first time a new dimension of aggression, dominance, and war-making on a grand scale, when power politics, empire building, and accumulation of wealth reached new proportions.

From the point of view of spiritual development, we tend to look down upon the Bronze Age preoccupations with power and dominance as less worthy, yet at that time they were sacralized, held in awe apparently for the reason that, being still new and unfamiliar, they were mysterious. Just as in individual development, so in cultures any new components of psychic evolution make their appearance first in archetypal expression with the aura of sacrality about them. Several centuries after the Bronze Age, in many cultures of the Near and Far East, the entire myth-and-ritual configuration was restored to its place of origin in the interior life of the individual.[5] Instead of the sacral king's role of holding accountability for the moral welfare of the entire populace, individuals now became responsible for their own. Each accomplished individual had to go through his own renewal and transformation of outlook.

In the new developments of that later time two issues were being worked out. One was the aforementioned restoring to the interior life of the psyche the Center that had been projected out and concretized. The other was that at the time the ethical system was being transformed, making it the task of the individual citizen to fulfill himself, just as the sacral king had once carried that role himself ritually as the ideal image of the fulfilled person. With this spiritual turn, violence became looked down upon as less worthy and as dangerous to the welfare of humanity, even as evil. Compassion and living together in brotherhood were envisioned as the preferred way to organize society on a quite different principle than law, policing, and coercion from the top. This new ethic was now seen as sacred and as a quality to be cultivated by spiritually developed individuals: this was caring concern for others, which had been known before principally as an attribute of the sacral kingship.

In my opinion, the key to an understanding of these cultural changes is to be found in the work of visionary experience. The prophets and seers who proposed this democratization of the myth and ritual of kingship were visionaries who perceived in myth-making a new possibility that developed the individual's moral sense, rather than entrusting such order to the leaders of society on the collective level. Visionary states are myth-making states.

Many persons today have had experiences of various kinds of altered states of consciousness, whether in meditation or at least in dreams, and have emerged from them with a new recognition of the character of the world, whether of nature or the spirit. In the deepest of such states, one spins out an original myth-form, describing the interior dynamics of one's most profound motivations. In a process of this dimension a new world-image is at the very center. In myth and ritual since the Bronze Age this world-image has taken the form of a quadri-partite circle, a mandala. This cosmic diagram, centered and dividing the surrounding space into four quarters, was a representation of the world and of the inner world of the psyche at the same time. Our own interior Center the "Self," portrays itself in this fashion in the form of a world-image that lies at the heart of a world outlook. Just as the Center in ritual form extended itself out into the structure of the kingdom, so in the psyche the Center unfolds into a system of functions by which we experience our world. Our inner Center is not only concerned with self-fulfillment, by which we come to an expanded and improved self-image or a concept of what we are and what our identity is. Such selfhood, when it becomes explicit, also is a way of interpreting the world and a manner of living in it, especially of living in society.

We must constantly remind ourselves that religions of the early urban culture, with all their elaborate myth and ritual, concerned them-selves primarily with government and were focused on the sacral king-ship. That was the manner in which the ancients used to give expression to inner psychic contents, seen most eloquently in the writings of the Taoists and Confucians in China.[6] These wise men equated one's pro-gress in spiritual cultivation to one's development of the capacities required for functioning harmoniously in society, or governing the people in fruitful accord with the Way of Nature.

The most telling picture of the psychic Center sees it as a con-densed set of possibilities awaiting actualization. The image comprises all the potentials for a value system, a system of meanings and understanding, a belief system and a design of life, all amounting to a cultural design compacted into this rather condensed mandala image. To use a familiar analogy from the old adage, one could say that just as the acorn in its tiny space contains all the potential of the unfolding of a huge oak, so the little mandala one might draw on paper or paint similarly has the capacity to develop and grow into a full range of consciousness, differentiating itself into very specific, explicit forms. Somehow the quality of the mandala then establishes the quality of the total outlook that is going to result afterwards.

On this account, "interpreting" any such image is not quite to the point; it is more helpful to encourage the expectation that the image will keep unfolding its meaning as it participates in an ongoing process, especially in a very active acute "psychosis." For example, when some-one enters upon the episode feeling that she is dying and that she is back at the beginning of time, I see the death image as almost always signifying the death of the limited state of being, of the previous state of the ego, or of the insufficient personality. It is an appalling experience to undergo when it actually is a "death trip." The expression is no mere simile or figure of speech; it is an actual coming to the end of something and not knowing at all what is ahead. One only knows that one is simply losing many familiar ways to which one has become accustomed, having no idea what is going to appear to replace them. Hence the experience really is like death, but it concerns the self-image, and hand in hand with that it becomes also the death of the world-image.

The visionary images that one sees might be similar to those that led to the famous Ghost Dance, starting on our West Coast at the close of the last century among the Amerindians. These visions[7] started with a prophet, a Paiute whom I will describe in chapter 9, standing one day on a mountain and beholding the whole earth opening like a great chasm with the known world falling into it; all creation disappeared for three days, at which point a new ideal world unfolded. The consequent myth and ritual then became the program for renovating the Amerindian society, for which they had great hopes. Similar accounts are given of the cargo cults in the Pacific Islands,[8] also envisioning the collapse of the known world as a prelude to its regeneration.

The destruction of the world in a great apocalypse is the opening theme in the making of many new myths. The cataclysm is the destruction, of course, not of the physical world, but of the way of perceiving the world, portraying the dissolution of the culture as it has been known up to that time. In times of cultural stress and dissonance accompanying rapid change, when the society must renovate itself and transform into a new configuration, myths are required to serve as guidelines and channels for the new energies needed in changed circumstances, with still unfamiliar problems to solve. Wallace has described these as "revitalization movements"[9] and La Barre, as "crisis cults."[10]

In reading the history of these cults and the transformations of the culture, one finds that these leaders went through experiences that today we would diagnose clinically as "acute psychosis." Yet such prophets would emerge from their trance with the myth that had been in the process of formation during those weeks (usually six, i.e., forty days) and the process would then be acknowledged as visions demonstrating the giftedness of such persons and their myth-making capacities.

Our clients are, of course, not necessarily potential prophets or reformers, but the underlying process is the same as theirs. The acute episode is an intensely creative myth-making, a preparation for starting over again with a new way of looking at things, each time with a different meaning for each individual. The death of the old self accompanied by the death of the old world-image represents the demise of the previously held culture-form. Simultaneously the opposites are constellated and clash with each other. The individual is in conflict, ethically and morally, in her value system, in such fashion that she sees two sides to almost any question that arises. The actual content of such conflicts is usually found to concern the psychic level of one's personal culture-form.

In doing therapy we learn to develop a way of taking our cues from the imagery, the ideation, not interpreting it prematurely, but listening for the life substance in it, that is, the life issues that surround the images. We encourage the individual to stick with these issues and work them out. In this way we find that even with cases of acute psychosis we are dealing from day to day with true psychotherapy, in considerable depth and in a highly dynamic process.

The most impressive and richest set of ideation is found in the messianic calling and its program. It is all too easy to dismiss these ideas as naive and inflated world-reforming idealism, such as one finds in the enthusiastic imagination of an adolescent. I must confess that for the first ten years of work with acute episodes I tended toward just this dismissal; I found myself bordering on impatience and diverting my attention. By now, on the contrary, I find that the messianic mission with its program for society represents the very essence of the person's needs for living in society with any satisfaction. The images picture the kind of culture the particular individual requires, thus offering a glimpse of the direction the psyche is attempting to move in its value system, and in its way of reading its experience and life in a social setting. "Interpretation" is in that case somewhat beside the point, but filling out the outlines, placing the clay on the armature or flesh on the bones, reaching the life experience that is hinted by these images, all become ways to foster the healing process.

What, then, is healing in the manner of therapy presented here? When someone enters an altered state of consciousness, particular kinds of phenomena occur as the energy drops down into the unconscious. One finds oneself in touch with cosmic concerns, mystical experiences hover nearby, and many manifestations of transpersonal phenomena occur, such as synchronicities and parapsychological perceptions; most of all, one is ready to see the world as one. This vision of oneness is expressed in the messianic ideation, along with the recognition that the world is going to be marked by a style of living emphasizing equality and tolerance, harmony and love. This hope is almost universally seen in persons in the acute episode.

When the psyche is strongly insisting on the visions of such a world, what is required is some setting in which the specific subculture matches them. In designing Diabasis what we did about this was to model it as closely as possible on that cultural program: we should establish a truly democratic structure, in which no one is boss but everyone is brother and sister in a large family, and in which it is safe to be loving and open with each other. In such an atmosphere persons can live in a truly psychological mode, not afraid to reveal angers and hurts, fear and distress. This warm and healthy style of living was sensed by any new client upon arrival within the first half-hour.

In this warmly humane setting, when a client would find herself with two or three staff members with whom she felt particularly close, the psychic Center would invisibly continue to carry on its deep work, accompanied by feelings of mutual exchange and caring. There would occur a steady breaking down of the pernicious interface produced by invalidation, and consequently its replacement by a dynamically creative one. Relationships of this kind were genuinely caring, not in the sentimental but the true sense.

This way of life in Diabasis I take to be representative of developments waiting to come about in the collective society of our time.[11] The new motivations arising from the deep psyche are voiced through many spokespersons who reveal information from its inner recesses concerning present societal trends. As the need for a new cultural set becomes felt, in whatever degree of crisis, this expectation can be trusted: the psyche knows what is needed and has sure and resourceful ways of handling the predicament and of finding the direction to take toward a fruitful future.

Chapter 6

Psychological Methods

Considering all that is being pointed out in this discussion, it becomes evident that among the extreme forms of visionary states there are certain ones that should not be handled by the customary regimens of medication and enhancement of skills, however much consensual reality and normative thought processes may have been lost. I will give a brief view of what is possible with an acute eruption of the psyche in "psychosis" when it is allowed to proceed in its own way to a fruitful outcome.

For illustrative case material I have had to reach back to my early experiences in the 1950s.[1] Because the immediate medication of psychotic episodes is universal today, it has been impossible to gather such accounts in the recent decade, and listening to a person's subjective preoccupations and ideations is usually not allowed in inpatient services nowadays. This custom of medicating and prohibiting listening is a great obstruction to the profession's education and research. Since what I pointed to earlier applies to my own teaching experience, I will repeat it now. It means that an entire generation of professionals coming through their training will never have had an opportunity to hear what goes on within the psyche of individuals in this state after the first day of admission; even when it is heard at the start, it is considered only for diagnostic purposes. The teaching is then done by psychiatrists who have never heard what the psyche does in the weeks following admission and thus who quite naturally dismiss the "mental content" as irrelevant.

In the late 1950s, in the county psychiatric facility I selected a thirty-year-old woman to work with who was in her first acute psychotic episode. Her start in life had been made difficult because of her abandonment by both parents: the father through death, and the mother through a mental crisis for which she had to be hospitalized.

When I introduced myself to her a couple of days after admission, she was in seclusion and in four-point restraints. I sat quietly on the corner of her bed and invited her to tell me what was going on, to which she readily replied that she was going through the whole story of the

New Testament and felt herself really to be there, experiencing the life of Christ. After some little talk with her about this story, I offered to come in every other day and talk with her about if it she wanted. The next time I came to see her she was still in restraints and so heavily medicated that she could hardly get her voice up to talk. I sat as before while she tried to express, in her quite clouded state, her religious concerns and her wish to reach out to me, feeling the sleeve of my tweed jacket and its texture. Touch of this kind I had long since found to be of great significance to persons in this state. This manner of encounter seemed to open the way for her to communicate to me her sense of mission to rewrite the New Testament, since it was going to be experienced all over again, with a particular emphasis on love in the world.

With our getting off to this start I was able to anticipate, from my experience of other such cases, what her psyche was about to undergo: a process in great depth whose aim would be the mobilization of her potential for relating and loving in a new way. She was seeing this as the need of the world to live by a newly invigorated myth. My task would then be the simple one of encouraging from time to time any readiness in her to recognize that her expectations concerned her inner world and its own myth, about to unfold itself to her inner vision. Such thought forms were far from "mere fantasies"; they were powerfully dynamic images that were on the verge of refashioning her basic orientation to her outer world.

In this kind of work I do not set up "therapeutic goals" drawn from some codification of what is "normal." For the psyche has its own designs according to its knowledge of what it needs for a fulfilled life; I do best to follow its leads with complete trust in its capacity to reach its ends in its own way. In consequence I do not consider my interventions to be the effective agents of progress. Opening oneself in this way to the psyche's processes and allowing oneself to be led by them is at first difficult for anyone conditioned by medical education and method, in which one has become accustomed to giving orders and managing patients. A different mode is being called for, the receptive one

My most definitive act at the start was to discontinue her medication, and my most meaningful one was to be affirmatively responsive to her concerns. The result was that by the next visit a couple of days later she was up and active, being playful and mixing with others in high spirits. She was eager to talk with me and tell me what she was going through in her inner experience. Her mischievous play, though light-hearted, was often considered excessive and she would worry the staff by taunting them with her antics. The best policy was to forego the ideal law-and-order and take all of this in the same spirit of humor that it had for her, and not "square off" with her or oppose her with heavy authority. In this fashion it was possible to learn from her where the behavior came from, and thus know what meaning it had for her. Her lifelong self-image had been that she was the "oddball" in her family setting, feeling different and bereft of acceptance. She had learned therefore to "carry it off" with joking and "playing the zany part," clowning and teasing. Hence it behooved the staff to refrain from aggravating this lack of self-esteem by harsh discipline; that way nothing would have been learned. Hospital care tends in many ways to reenact the hurtful family scene of childhood, perpetuating that which the psyche is trying to throw off.

In our interviews held every other weekday we sat in a quiet room at a table, in such a way as to have it between us but cater-cornered, so that we could feel together and not on opposite sides of a barrier. On the space between us we had drawing and painting materials, and as is usually the case, the psyche would get to work and play with images much as a child might. With encouragement and attention given them, a running commentary started up as the pictures unfolded. In this way I was introduced into her inner psychic life directly. Her first such theme was the Nativity, the time being actually near Christmas, a good start for her proposed reenactment of the life of Christ and for her renewal process just then getting under way.

However, her first experience at the time of dropping into her visionary process at home had been a sense of dying, as is almost universally the case. Crucifixion motifs abounded. Also she had even an image of all the people having died except three women and one man, amounting thus to a world destruction to prepare it for a renewal, in much the same manner as the universal myth of the Deluge.[2] She had undergone another nearly universal experience in the beginning phase, that of returning to the beginning of time at the Garden of Eden, and simultaneously to that of her own life as a child. It is customary for the return to the creation and to childhood to occur together. In vision she beheld also the progress of the creation in the early development of mankind, with primitive people migrating over the continents all naked. When she arrived on the ward she perceived all the people around her to be in an afterlife state, since she had now entered the realm of death.

With this rush of vivid imagery the question arises, what does a therapist do in response? I find interpreting to be of little consequence, in contrast to what one might do in therapy with persons in ordinary states of consciousness; with those I would hold mutual discussions to throw light on the wealth of meaning in the psyche's representations, such as in dreams. With persons in nonordinary states the effort is geared toward encouraging the process to continue moving forward, and not clutter it with attempts to translate it all into rational formulations. It is much the same as the experience of poetry that comes from that deeper level, such as the late poems of Yeats;[3] to transpose the flow of metaphor into prose would be to miss the impact the poem is designed to create, thus defeating its purpose.

At the same time, however, it is essential that I should recognize the meaning in the flow of images. If I were to feel bewildered by this inner drama because it made no sense to me, the young woman would sense this instantly and become cautious about revealing anything, an eventuality that would lead to her sense of isolation and even to her own confusion. In such a predicament the most dreaded interface would take shape between her state of total immersion in her myth world and my recoil from it, clutching onto my preference for our mundane, consensual, familiar reality. If, on the other hand, I have arrived at the position of having heard this many times before, and so having granted that myth world a status of realness, she would sense it. Merely the look on my face would be enough to reassure her that it was safe to keep moving with her process. My part here was therefore to convey my true sense of recognition of what was going on in her, by an alert interest in it, engagement with it, and encouragement of it. I also was indeed interpreting in my own thoughts, silently, and I believed that might have contributed to a gradual ordering of what had started in chaos.

In this spirit, then, I understood her death experience, and her sense of residing in an afterlife state, to express the shift in her focus of awareness away from the ordinary level of ego functions and outer reality and into the nonordinary state, with its psychic functions and inner reality composed of myth forms. She was overwhelmed by these deep processes. As already mentioned, death customarily expresses the demise of the accustomed self-image, while the world-destruction motif represents the collapse of the familiar cultural set. This way of understanding derives from the observation of this world-image in many cases, making it clearly evident that it concerns the issue of cultural and political ideologies.

In the renewal process, with world destruction and regeneration motifs[4] there is usually an accompanying conflict of opposite forces representing the upholding of one's culture against the subversive agencies that might bring it down. In this clash one's own personal, internal culture is in a process of transformation in terms of the world-image. In her visions she saw the world divided into two hostile halves threatening each other with destruction, and saw herself as situated at the midpoint between these factions. The good people were the Christians wanting to make use of her knowledge, the bad were the Communists plotting against her and planning to launch an invasion.

In this schema of cultural events the image of the Center was prevailing, as it does customarily in these types of visionary experiences. She was at the Center in the figure of the Garden of Eden in the creation process. Here she identified with the Center as the midpoint between opposing world factions. This position gives a glimpse of what the paranoid mechanism is made of. As William Allenson White pointed out long ago,[5] paranoid fears are associated with an often concealed megalomania; I would add that this inflation is usually expressed as being identified with the image of the Center, as is the case here.

Paranoid ideation is mainly of two kinds. There is the "paranoid personality," which tends to project any threatening images out and keep them out and disowned, perceived often as government agencies that are persecuting oneself in one way or another. This represents an attention style that in Julian Silverman's formulation[6] is "outward," associated with field-dependency, stimulus augmentation, and extraversion. However, "paranoid trends" occur in almost all cases of acute episode, by which one tends naively either to identify with the images that occur or project them out. Identifying and projecting are concretizations of a sort, though different from those seen in formal "thought disorders."

If by disposition one is fortunately endowed with the capacity to experience these images inwardly, with an "inward" attention style, one can readily turn the experience of the images around and recognize them as expressions of one's inner psychic processes. It usually does not require heavy persuasion with this inwardly oriented kind of person to be reminded of this fact and so to find oneself in the throes of an inner journey, instead of a nightmarish wandering through a world crowded with dangers. Silverman demonstrated this during our Agnew Project[7]—the ten subjects who emerged from their psychosis with the best outcomes were those who had been scored as showing the most definitively inward attention style.

It is the naive projecting of psychic contents that makes something a "paranoid delusion" that otherwise might be more profitably perceived as an encounter with one's own internal contradiction, the part of oneself that has been denied and is activated to make itself known. There is another manifestation of this kind of concretizing of imagery that should be realized symbolically and recognized as part of one's psychic development: this is the tendency in the psychotic state to identify naively with almost every image that happens to cross the stage of awareness. This is the feature par excellence that makes the mental content sound insane and offend the rational mind. To throw some light on this point, I am going to paraphrase the next array of images in this person's episode to render them as visions that she beholds rather than personages that she becomes.

She beheld the divine Creatrix, the creator goddess, fashioning stars and the moon and populating the world. She beheld the whole universe as a personification of this creator goddess who makes worlds and peoples. She saw old Mother Earth herself. A new Virgin Mary appeared, signifying a divine image being activated to provide her rebirth, and she had a vision of the Nativity in a stone grotto (actually standing outside her window). In fact she identified with each and every one of these great beings, making her statements sound grossly intolerable!

These visionary images are highly inflating and give the impression of being so megalomanic that they convey the sense of being truculent hybris rather than religious. The hall-mark of the religious attitude is a reverence for the majesty of the great beings of the spiritual world. One is then filled with awe for these numinous beings, and "creature-conscious-ness"[8] leads to humility in the face of them, a virtue much emphasized in spiritual disciplines. This young woman did indeed occasionally manifest this kind of attitude. Her attempt to portray the 23rd Psalm[9] in a painting was filled with just such an atmosphere: she kneels "beside the still waters," her hair falling in a reverse S shape, the same manner as in other paintings of herself kneeling in reverence before the Crucifixion. She holds in her hands a moonlike crescent showing that her "cup runneth over." The contents vaporize into a large ark circulating behind her, upward and around leftward to its descent in front of her in the form of a dove of the spirit. The depiction is done with care and considerable reverence for the transformative process indicated by the circulation of this substance.

This expression of reverence brings to mind the first of many such cases that I have studied and reported.[10] That young woman after having taken her own death experience as part of momentous world events, realized at Easter time that it was really Christ who died and was resur-rected, a great being, and not she herself, "only a little bit" in contrast— thus establishing a healthy relation to the mythic image. Disidentifying was part of her healing process.

Returning now to our case under discussion, only slightly less grand among the young woman's myth-styled images was that of the King and Queen in union. These were represented by the figures of Queen Elizabeth and "Perry Prince of Peace"; in myth and ritual this motif is familiar as the royal "Sacred Marriage," an integral part of the annual renewal rites of antiquity under discussion.[11] The Prince of Peace is a title of King James, whose name is given to the version of the Bible that he sponsored. There was, needless to say, a warm transference sustained throughout those weeks, beginning even on the first encounter between us.

Here we are reminded that however much there might be personal feelings in the relationship, they are founded upon this archetypal base in a typical myth-and-ritual image, forming an essential part of the renewal process. They are consequently not to be met with protests and corrections on the part of the therapist, but sustained comfortably without anxiety, in the expectation that she will find her own way to take the images as symbolic when she is ready to. On the first appearance of these feelings at Christmas time, she wrote a letter to Santa Claus asking for "a tweedy teddybear with a tweedie tie, with his chuckle buckle belt," a delightful childlike bit of humor meant to tell me how she felt. The note showed earmarks of the language of these deep levels, rhyming, punning, and alliteration with rhythmic cadence; these are not symptoms of disorder, but the deep psyche's natural way of expression,[12] giving rise to poetry when it reaches a sophisticated level of communication.

One day she brought a painting that she had done between interviews. It was of the crucifixion of a crowned serpent, with knife blades surrounding it and pointed toward it. Upon my asking what the serpent meant to her, she said it was just the one on the nurse's badge, only that; so I let it go at that time. Some days later she was involved in a story of what is happening to the earth by our violation of it. She said she knew that Mother Earth is angry with us and wants us to give back the metals that were wrested from her belly, stolen from her for our ill uses. She insisted we should give up the sciences and heavy industries and convert all the buildings used for them into homes, where we should grow our own food and lead lives with our families and personal relationships. It came to me at that point what that earlier crucifixion of her caduceus serpent had implied, and I asked if that was what she had meant. This suggestion released an angry tirade, lasting several sessions, about the evils of her own nursing profession and the medical sciences in general. Puzzled, I wanted to know why she was so vehemently enraged over this issue, and bit by bit it came to light that it was because her mother, with whom she had lived, had pushed her into the role of the man of the household, treating her as if she was a husband.

There is a wealth of significance in these concerns. One is that she made clear that what was being sacrificed was a self-image that she found damaging to herself as a woman. In consequence her visions portrayed a world cleansed of the masculine; all men but one had died in it, and all concerns of science and industry, which were seen as belonging to the masculine principle, were purged away. The crowning of the serpent suggests kingship and as already noted, my studies of the myth-and-ritual parallels to this kind of renewal process have shown that in ancient times the sacral kings were personifications of the cosmic and world Center. Fighting against world destruction and for its regeneration were the business of the rites of renewal of king and kingdom. It was her self-image, therefore, that was going through a transformation in terms of the fate of her Center.

Another striking significance is to be found by taking note of the simultaneous occurrence of the change in the self-image and the world-image, illustrating the transformation of the self going hand in hand with that of the subjective culture. As it comes into play it is endowed with specific ideologies assigned to its several segments.

In response to both the newly emerging self-image and world-image, it is vitally important for the therapist to be prepared to give full recognition to the various manifestations of the feelings of new selfhood and of changes in her gradually shifting cultural preferences. This recognition asks not for some intellectual concepts so much as for affirmations in terms of feeling. This person's visions were in tune with the collective cultural trends that at that time were just ahead in San Francisco, notably her sacrifice of the prevailing male dominance and her exaltation of the feminine values and preferences, accompanied by cosmic-size visions of Gaia and the Divine Creatrix. It would be difficult to deny validity to these images that were so appropriate both to her own life and to the cultural change gradually emerging in the world of our time.

A remarkable feature of this young woman's visions of the supremacy of the goddess, the return to the land, and the pulling down of the masculine establishment, is that she experienced them in 1958, a decade before the very same views became the myth around which an entire counterculture took shape in San Francisco. Visionary experience is by its very nature countercultural since it aims at transformation. These kinds of observations were what led me into my extensive studies of culture change and the role of prophets and reformers; these were endowed with the capacity to perceive and articulate the needed new myth and rituals for their cultures, most frequently becoming overwhelmed by their visionary state and caught in the throes of what most psychiatrists today would diagnose as a "psychosis." Yet they are "the movers and shakers of the world forever it seems," as Arthur O'Shaughnessy put it.[13] In some other cultures more spiritually oriented than ours, persons like this young lady are considered holy and given great respect, not pronounced sick or locked up. I am not suggesting that all persons in this "psychotic" form of visionary state should be considered prophets, but rather that the program of the visionary experience and its imagery is the same in well-known "prophets" as in our little-known "patients."

The sequence of visions in this young woman's process found its climax in a final one that displayed much of the prophetic spirit. She saw San Francisco as the New Jerusalem[14] initiating a whole new world order. A palace of gold marked the Center not only of the sacred city but even of the whole transformed world. There stood also the Tree of Life "whose leaves were for the healing of the nations." Not only would the culture be healed but a New Heaven and New Earth were to come into being, all in the phrasing of the Book of Revelation portraying the Apocalypse.[15] An era of peace and love was to follow as the fruit of this transformation of the creation.

The visionary state had by now done its work and reached its culmination. That the image at the end depicted a resolved state is verified by the circumstance that she herself was, in the clinical phrasing, "recovered," and in good spirits.

Part II

Chapter 7

Jung's Approach

We have seen that the crucial problem of the acute "psychotic" episode is, in essence, the judgment that society brings down upon outbreaks of the nonrational, and that when this label is lifted from the so-called patient, in these kinds of "psychosis" the signs and symptoms of insanity very soon go into remission by themselves.

A most eloquent expression of this issue is made by Theodore Roszak in *Where the Wasteland Ends*:[1]

> To be mad, as the world judges, is to be trapped in a narrow and lonely reality. To be sane, as the world judges, is to be trapped in a reality no less narrow, but heavily populated. But there is also the higher sanity, which is neither the going consensus nor the latest compensatory excess.
>
> Its health is freedom from all traps; its sign is the knowledge of many realities. All realities are real: but (the higher) sanity's reality is vaster, more various, more vividly experienced in all sectors, and more judiciously ordered.

Jung, of course, always maintained the position that schizophrenia was a psychopathology, and never refrained from regarding it as a mental disorder, with possibly a chemical basis. However, he was the first to state that it contained nature's efforts to heal, that what one witnessed on the wards was largely an artifact of hospitalization and its methods, and that schizophrenia was amenable very frequently to psychotherapy. His early essays on various aspects of psychology all laid the groundwork for the trends of the 1970s in the formulation and management of the acute episode. It is always to be borne in mind that Jung's lifework sprang at first out of his explorations of schizophrenia and that his first two masterworks were both on this topic.[2]

Twenty-five years ago the newly emerging view of psychosis began to change toward regarding the acute episode not as psychopathology but as an "altered state of consciousness," as a "crisis in growth and development" of such proportions as to throw the psyche into a "high-arousal state."

In the Jungian model these high-arousal states are regarded as activations of the deeper functions of the psyche, that is, the archetypal affect-images that are the dynamic foci of meaning and emotion, activated when the stresses of the personality or of the culture are such as to create an urgent need for a new orientation. Those that we see in ordinary practice are lesser versions of mental states that are written in the large in the careers of the great visionaries and prophets in various cultures who, in times of crisis, experience and express new myth forms that often have become capable of renovating their cultures, which had fallen into the stress state of cognitive and affective dissonance.

This picture of altered states and visionary states in the intense experience of rapid culture change gave me a new impression of what is happening in the myth forms experienced in the acute "schizophrenic" states. The reorganization that has presented itself again and again in these forms that I have encountered has basically consisted of a dramatic shift from affect-images of power and the Logos principle to those of relatedness and the Eros principle. This same shift we have found in the great myth-and-ritual forms of archaic cultures that produced the urban revolution with its heavy power mode, and a short time later, the age of the great prophets and philosophers, who proclaimed the virtues of the Eros way of life and its spiritual cultivation.[3]

The history of visionary and mystical states in the more developed cultures suggests that they activate this "receptive mode" that motivates us to relate sensitively and caringly toward our fellow beings.

The processes occurring in depth in the psyche can only be understood within the framework of the general historical setting. Jung made a point of this in his studies of medieval nature philosophy. In *Psychology and Alchemy*, he says about psychotherapy:[4] "Even when the patient believes himself quite unprejudiced (in respect to philosophical outlook) the assumptions underlying his thought, mode of life, morals, and language are historically conditioned down to the last detail."

The same holds true for the investigator of psychology. Jung stood at the threshold between a rationalistic era, in which nature was seen in a Newtonian, deterministic, and materialistic-positivistic terms, and our era, which is revolutionizing our understanding of the world of matter and energy, of the body, of the psyche, and of our natural environment. Roszak in his book traces the transition in the modes of scientific thinking. In the early heyday of the scientific outlook, thinking was purged of any elements that might suggest the nonrational, and purified its reasoning in order to gain mastery and control over nature and power over her processes. For example, Locke urged that "figurative speech serves but to insinuate wrong ideas, move the passions, and thereby mislead the judgment."[5] Descartes, too, maintained that "whether awake or asleep, we ought never to allow ourselves to be persuaded of the truth of anything unless on the evidence of our reason . . . , not of our imagination or our senses."[6] Imagination in this instance means forming images to combine and synthesize the data of our senses—that faculty that Einstein later found indispensable in creative scientific thought process. All this Descartes declared despite his own experience of discovering the new laws of mathematics through a visionary state, that is, as a revelation from the visitation by an angel![7]

The romantic era registered its protest against such constraints of the mind. Roszak reminds us what a standard-bearer Blake was, proclaiming that "Enthusiastic Admiration is the First Principle of knowledge and its last." Imagination for Blake was a divine principle.[8]

The splendid culmination of this cultural shift came in the person of the poet-scientist Goethe. Over against the "domineering analysis" of the rationalistic hard sciences, he preferred the "passive attentiveness," which we would recognize as the "receptive mode." As Roszak puts it, "he had a sharp eye for the unique moment, the astonishing insight, crowning perhaps years of waiting . . . getting into the swing . . . gradually, patiently, receptively, even as we get to know-by-loving and love-by-knowing."[9] With an "inner eye that sees the underlying ideas" in nature, Goethe said of his way: "By contemplation of an ever-creative nature . . . had I not myself ceaselessly pressed forward to the archetype, though at first unconsciously, from an inner urge; had I not even succeeded in evolving a method in harmony with nature?"[10]

Early in his career Jung revealed the many affinities he had with Goethe, who he thought might be his biological ancestor but was at least his spiritual forebear. In the two years after his break with Freud, he published four essays that delineated his basic point of view and his method of observation and therapy. I consider it to be these that made possible his whole new look at the problem of schizophrenia and also our own different way of viewing and handling it today.

The first essay, "Two Kinds of Thinking," in his *Symbols of Transformation*,[11] is his introduction to a study of the symbols in the diary of a schizophrenic girl. The remarkable feat in this essay is that he gives equal validity to both the active rational mode and the nonrational receptive mode, spelling out how this is justified.

The first mode is called directed thinking; it is the logical reality-thinking whose function it is to adapt to the outer world. It imitates "the successiveness of objectively real things" in images that follow one another in the same causal sequence as the events they represent. This operates under directed attention, uses language to communicate, and becomes an instrument of culture for control and mastery of nature by making use of freely disposable psychic energy.

The second mode is called nondirected thinking, which leads away from outer reality into fantasy images of the past and of the future. It is effortless, spontaneous, and is guided by the motives of the unconscious with contents that have become activated and lie ready to hand. Where directed thinking copies reality and tries to act upon it, nondirected thinking turns away from reality and sets free the subjective tendencies that are not productive of adaptation. Rather than trying to understand the real world as objectively and accurately as possible, it seeks to adapt that world to the subjective fantasies and expectations. This renders a picture, then, of a "universe completely removed from reality" but exactly corresponding to the image of man's subjective fantasy. This mode is apt to be designated as "infantile" or even "pathological." However, it is more accurately described as the "archaic" mind, which makes its first appearance onto the psychic scene in childhood.

In the early 1970s psychophysiological research into the function of the brain began to validate this concept of two co-equal modes of consciousness represented in the activity of the left and right hemispheres.[12] The left is the seat of active and directed functioning, with the faculties of speech and logical processing of data, and with sharply differentiated perception. The right is the area handling the receptive mode, which processes data in a holistic manner, and the paralogical thought process, that is, thinking via image, symbol, and metaphor.

Jung's validation of the subjective viewpoint in his initial discourse was enlarged and amplified in an essay following soon upon it. "On Psychological Understanding"[13] was written together with his first attempt at dealing with the problem of defining an energic concept of the libido, "On Psychic Energy,"[14] and they were meant at first to be companion pieces. Both are highly sophisticated approaches to the problems of theory by examining the standpoint of the observer. The only possible hope for generally valid theories is to take account of the psychology of the psychologist's viewpoint.

Jung pointed to two opposing but fundamental ways of viewing psychological experience, the prospective and the retrospective views. Where the retrospective deals with material in an "analytic-reductive" fashion, the prospective does so in what Jung termed a "synthetic-constructive" method. The former, for example, seeks to reduce a symbolic statement, like a poem, to its determining factors, whereas the latter wants to discover what the poet means by his metaphorical expressions.

Where the reductive explanation analyses the complicated symbolic product to its simple causes (in one's history) and to general principles (of dynamics), the constructive way explains by observing the living effect of the symbolic expression upon the subject, and keeps it alive and creative as it builds toward higher and more differentiated firms moving toward unknown but individual goals. The analytic view has the satisfaction of achieving a more objective understanding, whereas the other gives special validity to the subjective meaningfulness.

Jung cites the delusional system of Schreber, about which Freud had written his famous formulation of the paranoid mechanism from the reductive point of view. Jung presented the other way of understanding this from the constructive viewpoint, which does not look upon the imagery as infantile or pathological only. He saw Schreber as consumed by a desire to create world systems, which can only be understood as efforts to enable the individual to assimilate newly activated unknown psychic phenomena and thus to find a way of adapting to his own inner psychic world, a subjective adaptation. It amounts to a stage on the way to adapting the personality to the world, a stage that is characteristic of the type of personality that needs a previous conceptual formulation of the world, a preliminary philosophy before feeling at home in it.

About the necessity to such an individual of having his visionary experience validated, Schreber himself was eloquently forceful: after stating that the person in the normative state is "mentally blind" compared with one who is not and who receives "supernatural impressions," he writes in his Memoirs: "He is therefore as little likely to persuade the visionary of the unreality of his visions as a person who can see will be persuaded by a really blind person that there are no colors."[15]

Jung's essay first keynoted the approach that later became characterized as the "growth" or "developmental crisis" model. That is, this model viewed the activation of the nonrational and unconscious contents and the consequent turmoil as part of the psyche's effort to reorganize for further growth.

The companion piece to this essay on psychological understanding—also first written in 1914 but not published until years later—dealt with the sticky problem of how to assess the energies of the psyche and formulate them in a way that did them justice. Here again Jung noted that the standpoint of the observer leads him to the selection of what he sees and to the conclusion that he draws. Thus a preference for the objective viewpoint leads one to conceive energy in a concretized form as it is embodied in the play of "forces," such as specifically sexual libido or a power drive. The subjective outlook, however, requires that one perceive energy as primarily a mental concept, as a pure system of relations of energetic values, thus framed in a quantitative mode rather than a qualitative one that sees only specific energic forces. Conversions and transformations of energy can be well accounted for in this conceptual framework that deals with pure energic relations and with the symbols and processes that effect these changes. The role of the symbol then is to operate as a device for transforming energy. This is a statement that can be made only in a context that sees purposive and aimful activity in the unconscious processes. From this point of view, also, energy can be seen to be generated by a play of opposites that sets up natural polarities and shifts of gradients inducing the flow of energy.

This hypothesizing of a psychic energy then leads into a most significant formulation of the process of regression. We have already reviewed the concept of two kinds of thinking: directed, which serves adaptation; and nondirected which conforms to the conditions of the inner world, of fantasy, and of individuation. In terms of energy, forward movement serves adaptation; but if the prevailing attitude that governs it is no longer adequate to work, then there takes place a damming up of the libido. This then breaks up the pairs of opposites, which before had been united in their coordinated flow in the progressive direction; in their progressive aspect they lose their energic value, which instead shifts to the inner fantasy play as these opposites gather more and more associations. That is, all those psychic processes not concerned with adaptation increase with energic value; they tend to be underestimated because they do not serve the purposes of adaptation to the real world, but actually they lead instead to the necessity of adapting to the inner world of the psyche.

In this conception, then, progression sustains the process of adapting to the outer world and suppresses all the tendencies and possibilities subserving individuation, while regression does the opposite, adapting to the contents of the inner world and springing from the vital need to satisfy the demands of individuation.

It should be recalled in this connection that one of the more far reaching modifications of psychoanalytic theory in later decades has been Kris's formulation of "regression in service of the ego."[16] This new ego psychology has more than a few affinities with Jung's early work of three decades before, in particular the concept of the positive aspect of a regression that can serve the purposes of growth. The Jungian parallel to Kris's phrasing would be "regression in the service of the Self," that is, as part of the individuation process.

The remaining question, dealt with in another essay,[17] is that of a method for relating to these activated unconscious contents and bringing them into a fruitful working relation with the conscious and the unconscious, calling it "transcendent" because it serves to make a transition from one attitude to the other organically possible without the loss of the regulating influences from the deep psyche (the term has not a metaphysical but a mathematical derivation). In the therapeutic relationship the analyst mediates this function for the analysand by bringing together the factors from both conscious and unconscious levels. This view of the transference is again reached from the synthetic-constructive standpoint, which focuses not upon the historical antecedents alone, such as the parent figures, but upon him or her in respect to future development.

Again Jung in this discussion honors the inner process even when it might otherwise be depreciated as psychopathology and only its causes given attention. In the intensity of an emotional disturbance like depression, he points out, lies the energic value that the ego needs to have at its disposal for adaptation. The method is then to allow the fantasy to play freely but around the orbit of the affect. By focusing upon the mood, the play of imagery reproduces the content of the depression. This elaboration of the mood renders a picture of the tendencies of the unconscious, and becomes an enrichment and clarification of the affect. The emotion that has been unrelated becomes clear and articulate, and thus a new psychic situation is brought into being. This is the work of the transcendent function, and the method is that of "active imagination." The expression of the images then allows the unconscious to do its natural work of compensating for the biases of the conscious outlook; that is, the opposites are brought together so as to create a third expression that can embrace them, and this is also the transcendent function.

It is of central importance for this discussion that in formulating the transcendent function Jung pointed to the relation between the affect and the image. For in the therapy of schizophrenia it becomes apparent that the direction of the work of active imagination is opposite to that found in the depressive states. As Jung described it, the need for the depressive person is to let the affect produce its own images through actively concentrating upon the mood; so in schizophrenia we find an eruption of images that are overwhelming consciousness and that need to be given free play in order for them to lead to their natural affective components. In this condition the symbolic image is the avenue to the missing affect.

In these writings, published during his most formative years at the time of his separation from the Vienna school and establishing his own (1912–14, his age being 37–39), Jung was not merely conceptualizing in theories. The vein of the thought running through all of them reflects the essential quality of his nature, that of coming into relationship to that which he does not yet understand. His inclination was at every point to credit the subjective contents of another person's experience as having potential validity and value. In that way he became acquainted with the meaning of a panoply of subjective contents and processes through experiencing them by opening himself fully to them.

This unusually daring openness to the unknown that awaits in depth resulted from Jung's way of handling his own depth. These essays were written during the period when he was carrying on his own encounters and confrontations with the unconscious and was receiving from there many profound insights and connections with archetypal wisdom. He wrote of himself that the notations he made in these dialogues with the figures of the unconscious psyche provided him with the basic material that later became the substance of his psychology as worked out through observation and formulation. That is, his psychological model and theory grew out of the actual experience of actively relating to the psyche.

In this spirit Jung says of the psychotic productions as observed from the constructive standpoint:[18] "Here the delusional system, as regards its material content, is neither infantile nor in itself pathological, but subjective, and hence justified within these limits." This affirmation of the meaningfulness of the subjective fantasy-formation puts the finger on the essential point in his way of dealing with psychotic states, and it was fundamentally different from the then current psychoanalytic and psychiatric methods, and even from much that goes on in our present time. A subjective mental process can be scrutinized objectively, of course, but it can be judged justifiably only from its own subjective standpoint.

This establishes the ground, then for the specifically Jungian way of understanding psychotic experience. That way is epitomized in a surprisingly bold statement:

> The constructive method, true to its nature, must follow the clues laid down by the delusional system itself. The thoughts of the patient must be taken seriously and followed out to their logical conclusion; in that way the investigator himself takes over the standpoint of the psychosis.[19]

What a wildly daring and true directive for affirming and validating the efforts the psyche is making in the psychotic state to solve its problems! What could be more like Goethe's way of approaching nature, whereby "the knower must blend with the known unobtrusively," by "contemplation of an ever creative nature . . . pressing forward to the archetype" and succeeding in evolving a "method in harmony with Nature!"

In this manner Jung was faithful to the open-minded, receptive mode, the Eros principle that relates to what is there. Rather than imposing a conceptual scheme upon nature in order to have the mastery and control over it by rationalistic theories, he let his empathetic participation in the subjective experience of persons and historical eras speak their own meanings to him.

The effects of these attitudes and approaches show up clearly in the way Jung understood the psychology of the schizophrenic episode in the essays written during the years 1914–19.[20] I will not attempt to note all his work on the subject that followed later, but will concentrate on these few essays to indicate the clarity with which he could perceive the plight of the psychotic and also the aims that the psyche reveals in the acute episode.

In these several papers, on psychosis as such, he revealed his penetrating way of regarding this condition. He emphasized that by careful scrutiny of the emotional situation and the history of the individual the psychosis becomes comprehensible. The episode breaks out at the moment of some great emotion and consists of an intense and disturbing reaction to an emotional problem. In this sense no symptom could be called groundless or meaningless; rather, in the preoccupations lie the very foundations of one's being and the matrix of all the vital problems in which humans in general are engaged. There is a predisposition in such individuals to an abnormal sensitiveness that makes them differ from the ordinary person in conflicts, by an intensity that is all out of proportion to the circumstances. When there is no help found and no understanding, panic takes over with a flood of chaotic emotion and ideation.

With this entry into the making of the psychosis, Jung then perceived clearly the aim that it was motivated by. He recognized the compensatory role in the unconscious productions. Ordinarily, the unconscious effects compensations and balances that offer a natural corrective influence upon the biases and blindnesses of the conscious outlook. Ordinarily these are not so extreme that they go without effect. In the case of the psychotic, however, there is a characteristic refusal to recognize this effect, and an increased defensiveness against it. Then the pairs of opposites are torn asunder, creating deep division and disaster. The compensation that should be the beginning of a healing process, relieving the isolated conscious attitude, comes in a form so archaic and so violent that it becomes unacceptable to the consciousness of the individual. It largely becomes projected out and tends to form a paranoid system in which one feels abused or threatened.

Jung maintained clearly that the contents of the psychosis are not more abnormal than those of dreams. It is rather a condition in which the contents that were formerly unconscious take the place of reality. The individual loses hold of the concrete value of life and the unconscious takes the place of the real.

His study of the Miller fantasies in *Symbols of Transformation* was Jung's masterpiece,[21] rendering a full picture of the meaningfulness of the psychotic play of the primordial images, which he later defined as archetypes. These cover a wide range of imagery: the hero, the nurturant and the terrible mother, regression, sacrifice, death and rebirth, and the treasure hard to attain.

In my own work with psychosis my way of applying analytical psychology has been to follow not Jung's conceptual formulation of the schizophrenic "disorder" but rather the basic principles of his approach. These can be captured in their essence as affirmation and exploration, in the active aspect of the work, and attentive openness in the receptive aspect.

The emphasis on recognizing pathology and disorder is here replaced by validation of the inner process in which the individual is engulfed. In this way a relationship of trust is established that in time gives the individual an opportunity to emerge from a state of profound withdrawal.

With this validation there follows naturally the need to relate fully to what is happening in the individual's inner world. This is revealed to those persons whom the individual senses as having the ability not only to tolerate the nonrational material but also to understand and participate meaningfully in it.

Chapter 8

Relationship as Healing

If the therapeutic factors in the psychotherapy of the neuroses are puzzling, those in the psychoses are utterly mysterious. So much is this the case that in the average psychiatric opinion it is generally held that, as a matter of fact, there is no healing for the psychoses, that there can be alleviations of symptoms but not cure. I have always been reluctant to accept this closing of the door upon the possibility of healing, and that is because I find, as Jung has found, that the psyche knows better than we do what it is up to in its deep turmoils. There is much we do not know about these cataclysms, but we can at least point to areas to investigate.

For example, what is it that happens to the young lady mentioned earlier when, in a beginning psychotic state, she is admitted to a hospital ward and totally disintegrates into her delusions and hallucinations; she grimaces and postures but utters no words, and is so hostile and combative that she has to be put into bed restraints and shipped off the same day to a state hospital? On the other hand, when this same lady is transferred to our residence facility she becomes clear and coherent overnight, functioning in most ways quite naturally though still for a brief period a little resistive toward looking into her inner concerns. What is it that has transformed this picture so dramatically?

At Diabasis we were told by several of our clients that when they were first admitted into the community they took a careful look around, noted the faces and the bearing of the staff and sensed the atmosphere, and very quickly felt that they were safe to let go. Though on admission they were as psychotic as could be, usually they became clear and coherent within a matter of one to three days without medication.

It becomes quite apparent that in the psychosis something urgently needs to take place in the psyche, and also needs to come into relationship with someone. When a staff member declines to receive this experience, there occurs an appalling sense of thwarting, of the way being blocked; then ensues an upwelling of anger that shakes the individual's foundations. Madness is a state of being "mad" in both senses of the word. Various synonyms point to this state: furor, raging, berserk, amok.

Much that then occurs in a hospital setting turns out to be a host of indirect expressions of anger and resentment and frustration.

Since the psyche has its own intentions in a psychosis, when the unconscious is activated to this extreme degree, a welter of emotions wants to come into play, accompanied by images of a mythological cast that belong to these emotions. Most of these elements of the psyche are very necessary to the further growth and development of the personality. It becomes a very painful experience when they meet a wall of prohibition that dams up their flow and prevents their movement.

Our question is, then, what is it that goes on when psychotherapy does the other thing, allowing all the communications of affect and image to come through and be received into relationship? What is the nature of this therapeutic bond that makes it work toward reordering and reintegrating the psyche?

Speaking in very general terms, the intention of such therapy is to honor what the other person experiences with a readiness to receive her whole being, to relate to all that is in her, and thus to share in her psychic life and be in it with her during this critical period of growth. This entails attitudes of regard, respect, interest, concern, and partnership in the developmental process, with a full range of emotional experiences. Thus, as Jung has put it, psychotherapy consists of two whole psychic systems interacting in depth, in which action each is deeply affected by the other.

That is the overall view, and it may be seen under higher magnification if one asks oneself just what it is that one experiences as a therapist in this interaction.

When someone pours out her emotional experience to me, I am moved with that same emotion in empathy with it. This leads to my replicating in myself her experience with the emotions and images that belong to her psychology. By the same token, when I respond with my feelings to these recountings, the client replicates in herself my feeling experiences. Also, when I respond with my recognition of the meaning of her recountings, the client equally replicates in herself my understanding. The two modes are empathetic feeling and understanding clarity.

In this exchange, I develop in myself as a therapist a full range of information, of events, meanings, values, outlook, dreams, memories, and other items belonging to the full context of the client's life experience. Hopefully, all these arrive to lodge in my psyche without walls or blind spots that might shut them out. If so, I am accepting the full range of her life in a constellation as complete as her communications allow. The result is that I hold in my mind a growing mini-model of that person. So much is this the case that I find myself associating recent occurrences with past dreams and old events often more clearly than she. This is because I do not hold in myself the same resistances and defenses that she does, hopefully. It is up to me to see to it that I am open and without these walls. In that case, my client can assimilate my feeling responses and my cognitive understanding, and thus see things now freed from the walls, blocks, and resistances that might have been there toward these issues before. The image of the therapist becomes the model for her potentially free consciousness.

It is not unusual for clients to describe the somewhat uncanny sense of the therapist as a personal presence monitoring their consciousness from moment to moment (between sessions) as if sitting on their shoulder, looking on and commenting. Also it is common for me as therapist to have the sense, at the moment my client enters the room, of her bringing into it the atmosphere of the whole context of her life, as if wakening the dormant shadows of her near and distant past, with names, scenes, emotions, and images all springing to life. The intensity of this experience varies with the degree to which I have opened myself to that person, for that facilitates her opening to me. If she has met walls in me and "no take" on certain aspects of experience, there is distress and guardedness, leading to impoverishment of the exchange. Wholeness becomes then actualized in the fullness of the interchange.

The analogies here to the relation of loving feeling between two persons cannot escape the eye. It is very difficult for the profession of psychotherapy to know what to do with this awkward circumstance. The way to ease the tension around the issue has been from the beginning to take refuge in the fact of the "transference," which, holding vestiges of previous, parental relationships, minimizes the validity of the presently growing relationship that exists in its own right. The ardor that springs up has been made even more safe by perceiving it as the "transference neurosis," needing a lot of interpretation to keep it under control and finally to dispel it. A term that has been used for this effort is the graphic phrase, "crushing the transference," thereby telling the whole story in epitome.

These formulations were made more than seventy-five years ago, the space of three generations. Culturally, we now find ourselves in a different place in relation to these emotions. A certain restive objection prevails nowadays depending upon the cultural temper of any particular decade, against this rationalistic bias that seeks to interpret the transference feelings as anachronistic illusions and projections, allowing rather the possibility that the relationship's ardor has its own meaning and its own goals.

So far I am describing a state of the therapeutic relationship in which the therapist holds in her psyche a mini-model of the client, and the client in her psyche, a minimodel of the therapist. However, that is only part of the story of what occurs in such an interaction of two psyches. It is more or less the essence of what occurs on the personal level of the psychology of both persons. In a more profound and archetypal dimension, on the other hand, another configuration is at work that involves the image of the Center.

If the relationship between the two persons in the process is intimate and open, and each is communicating in an unguarded, authentic vein, then there begins to appear in dreams the image of the Center as a framework of the interaction. Jung has written much on this subject as the phenomenology of the "vessel" of the "opus," in the alchemical symbolism. All the elements of the inner process are poured into this retort and go through transformations as they combine and synthesize. Or the imagery might be that of the "temenos," the sacred enclosed space in which the mysteries are performed. This imagery does not spring merely from Jungian scholarly myth-making, but from the actual phenomenology of work with dreams in therapy.

A frequent dream expression of the relation between the two persons in this work, as I have seen it, is that of their working together on the creation of an object in the space between them. For example, a round tabletop is being carved by both parties jointly, fashioned in the image of a mandala of some sort.

The experiential aspect of this imagery, as I see it, is that all the content of the client's process, and all the responses of the therapist, meet and mingle in this mutual emotional field being established between the two persons. In this sense, the integrating effect is produced not only in the ego of the client, with her insights and awareness, and not only in the clarifications offered by the therapist, nor is it produced even only in the archetypal activity of the "Self" within the client's unconscious. Rather, it is in this vessel of the relationship between them. If the client is indeed opening up with all her experience, and the therapist is truly receiving it all with openness and without limiting blocks and walls, then all the dimensions of emotional, conflictual, and spiritual concerns in the client can be received into this vessel and processed there.

In this sense, integrating is done first in the vessel, first in the relationship, and only secondarily in the psyche of the client.

It is in this view the relationship that organizes and reorganizes experience. It is this that produces the dramatic effects so often seen in the interview. A client may come all in a turmoil of anxiety, pour it all out, and magically sense a relief merely in proffering these confidences.

A confidence is *con-fide*, an action of mutual faith with someone. It is given because there is the surety of knowing that one's experience is going to be honored and given full credit for the meaning that it holds, even when it is poorly understood or still unknown.

There are advantages in acknowledging the therapeutic relationship as one of loving feeling. Chief among these is that the emotional charge and heightened intensity induce at the same time a dramatic activation of the unconscious psyche in great depth, so that the archetypal affect-images become vivid and dynamic. They are stirred in this atmosphere of mutual trust and mutual enthusiasm. It is characteristic of love relations that the archetype of the Center is constellated between two individuals.

Much of the synthesizing and organizing action of the psyche goes on at the level of the unknown, that is, of unconscious process, long before it is a matter of conscious insight—long before it reaches the ego. This unconscious process is essentially emotional in its quality and hence the play of emotion is best allowed to do its own work. Too early a recognition of meaning, and formulation of it, may scotch this subtle process that goes on below the surface.

However, the image of the Center appears only when it will. It is one of the many elements that may be "projected" in the relationship, but also may not. The occurrence of the image of the Center is only one among several possibilities, and other unconscious contents may have to play themselves out in the "transference." However, in the acute "psychotic" episode I find the Center to be quite regularly represented as the focus of the whole process. Inasmuch as we are discussing at present the healing factor in this psychosis, it would be well to note some of the ways in which the image of the Center operates in psychotic ideation.

The central archetype is the factor in the psyche that, according to all the evidence in our observations, has the capacity to transform the self. This change involves not only the self-image in the usual sense, but also the structure of the personality as a whole. The means by which this is brought about in the psychotic episode are those that I have described as the "renewal process." When I speak of this kind of "ideation," it should not be thought of as a fanciful play of symbolic ideas. Rather, they occur as powerful, even overpowering, emotional and spiritual experiences. That is the reason for my preferring to refer to these archetypal phenomena as "affect-images," since they are made up principally of emotion and image together as aspects of the same entity.

To review briefly what has already been described, this process of renewal is ushered in by frightening feelings of death and of the world being threatened with destruction. Forces are believed to be aligned against one another, the one to bring about this annihilation of the universe—or at least of the moral and social order—the other to preserve it. Creation is experienced anew. However, if all goes well, the death leads but to a new birth, the world destruction to a renewed world-image, and the clash of cosmic or social powers to a new design of life and a new structure of values and meanings. A messianic image is brought into play whose role is to fashion and proclaim this new state of being-in-the-world.

There is a widely held view currently, among the very people who do the most open and receptive work with the therapy of this psychosis, that to maintain such a stance one must not have theories. The argument is that if one has intellectual expectations, these get in the way of the process that otherwise will go its own way and do its own work. There is considerable influence from Laing's writing in this regard.

In my experience, though, there is a quality of participation in the psychic process that is vital to the client. This is what I have spoken of as "informed listening," that is, hearing the client's communications with recognition of them from past experience. This may result either from one's own or from that of others who have recorded the actual occurrences that have taken place. In this regard I find autobiographical materials fully as valuable as the professional ones. The client in the psychosis knows immediately whether the things she is communicating are being found meaningful or incomprehensible. In this altered state it makes all the difference when her experience is being found not utterly bewildering but recognizable, for that releases her from the feeling of being isolated in her alienation.

One of the most important of the effects produced by informed listening has to do with the knotty problem of labeling. We have seen that the labeling can visibly be observed to have the effect of making the individual feel insane and, in consequence, be and act insane. However, the opposite may also be observed, that when the altered state is affirmed as being a perfectly valid mental space to be in, and possibly fruitful for spiritual and psychological development, the individual may quickly feel intact once more, and be and act quite coherent.

Each is a way of expressing one's evaluation of this state, and some sort of label remains necessary since the individual undergoing the experience needs to know what is happening in order to get some sort of working relation to it. Also a therapeutic staff need to be able to designate it. A more appropriate kind of label, then, should convey the significance of the actual process going on. The phenomenology of the episode has to do with death and birth, world destruction and recreation, and a play of opposites that at first clash but later become reconciled. I have not been able to think of a more benign label than "renewal process" as the name of the syndrome, and "visionary state" as a designation for the condition of mind.

From this vantage point, then, the process is being seen as having its focus not upon symptoms but upon the self-image with its root in the deepest and most dynamic layer of the psyche, that is, the central archetype of the "Self." It appears to be this factor, the self-image, that becomes transformed during the episode. I will indicate briefly how this seems to come about, as I have observed it:

Because of the hurts and emotional injuries in early years, the individual has learned to withhold from intimate, mutually open relationships with others. These might otherwise have brought into play the sharing of the Center in the manner I have been describing, but instead, the Center has tended to be experienced only in aloneness, in a sort of secret relation to it. The self-esteem is low and debased, and the archetypal image of the Self takes on a compensating function of overvaluing, with fantasies of the heroic or superlative "real" nature of oneself that is kept as a precious secret. The result is a psychology of defending one's prestige and power but not coming into close and revealing relations of affection.

The split self-image, too low on the ego-level, too high on the archetypal, in this way has gone without the corrective experience that would occur if there were frank interchange in intimate relationships. In this interior isolation, it takes only some blow to self-esteem, or some influx of intensity in feeling sensed as dangerous, for the whole balance to be upset and for the unconscious psyche to be roused into hyperactivity. This leads to the precipitation of the "high arousal state" in which the lower centers and functions are activated at the expense of the higher. Physiologically, it induces a high-stress or alarm reaction, which some psychiatrists see as the "cause" of the psychotic episode.

In my observations, the central archetype is the factor in the psyche that is extraordinarily activated in this psychosis. For all the reasons I have been mentioning, it is most difficult for the individual in this state to be left alone with it. If, on the other hand, the image content is brought into relationship, in the manner I have been suggesting, the sequence tends to move through the process that gives renewal to this central archetype of the Self.

The chief characteristic of the renewal, as I have mentioned, is that the potentials and capacities of the Eros principle are activated and made available for living. When that happens, then the old split self, heretofore kept in isolation, gets its chance to loosen up and come into relationship. The new form of the self leads to an emotional life capable of some richness of interchange, and to a sharing of experience of the Center with another.

This means that there comes through this process a new *valency*, so to speak, for relating in depth. This term is borrowed from chemistry but is also very apt for the psychology of relationship. In chemistry it means the quality that determines the number of atoms that a particular element may combine with, thus a readiness to unite. This readiness of the individual in the "psychotic" process to relate in depth imperatively requires a corresponding readiness of the therapist to do likewise. Both centers must be prepared to combine, again a chemical metaphor. When this does occur, the two centers become involved mutually and together undergo an experience of transformation. Things go well as long as the individual and the therapist are able to tolerate the play of the emotions that are released—rage, love, agony, exaltation, and so on—no matter how intense, as well as the play of all the imagery—mythic, religious, political, and so forth—no matter how unfamiliar.

Now in this full interchange I am pointing to affect and image as the two aspects of the process. The affect tends toward expression, toward conveying the high charge to someone so that it may come into relationship. The image renders the meaning of the affect to one's understanding. The personal style of a therapist may lead to emphasizing one of these two aspects at the expense of the other. There are those who tend to feel that the play of the emotion mutually in relationship is the "real" objective of the therapy, and those who are so fascinated by the richness of the symbolism in the process that comprehending it seems to be the "real" substance in the work. In the Jungian framework, these two modes belong to the general categories of experience that we call "Eros" and "Logos" respectively. Eros tends toward entanglement in experience in relationship, Logos toward abstracting out of experience the meaning and understanding. For balance and wholeness, both should come into play and receive their due.

Returning now to the original question asked at the start of this discussion—what happens in therapy that makes it work—it seems to me clear that only the readiness of the therapist to receive the whole of the client's experience and to relate to it and interact with it can suffice. Declining to do so seems to me only to thwart what nature is requiring for wholeness. The two effective virtues of therapy may be said to be *claritas* (clarity) and *caritas* (caring).

The mention of these two modes asks now for an investigation into their evolution in terms of their history in myth and ritual. (See appendix A for queries on this chapter and responses to the same.)

Chapter 9

Love and Power in Myth and Ritual

During the early phase of an individual's "psychotic" process, affect-images predominate that express themes of power, inordinate control, and supremacy over all else in terms of being a king, savior, or deity presiding over the world. There is characteristically a movement from that position of power to one that explores the potential for equalitarian and loving relatedness —that which in Jungian psychology is called the Eros principle.

The shift from fantasies of supremacy to those of relationship may find expression in terms of a messianic mission to bring love into the world, or perhaps a revolutionary move to upset a tyrannical order in favor of one with ideals of brotherhood. I think here of a Spanish-American woman who believed her grandfather to be the emperor of the Aztecs heading an autocratic and tyrannical regime. She was queen, but her four uncles overthrew the old man and divided the kingdom into four equal parts, over each of which one would rule by principles of equality, tolerance, kindness, and brotherhood.

Madness rouses a myth-forming, visionary state of the psyche in which the Eros principle becomes awakened. Because of centuries of fear of mad states and the consequent heavy prejudice against them, in our part of the world these are considered a rather dubious source from which to expect spiritual benefits to arrive. However, I want now to review briefly the qualities of other visionary states and show that indeed, it seems to be one of the goals of such states to reveal and activate the Logos and Eros principles.

These Logos and Eros principles are seen in Jungian psychology as categories or modalities of experience.[1] The Logos is that which abstracts from experience and discriminates and divides, for purposes of understanding and mastery. Science is the supreme example; the word itself means knowing, and in the West its early spokesmen stressed that its purpose was to master nature by understanding her laws.[2] When the Logos principle goes into action, it assumes the power motivation. Clear-headed objectivity is its manner.

Eros, on the other hand, is that which entangles in experience and relatedness, and which interweaves the data of experience into wholes. Eros prompts one to relate to beings as they are in their fullness, with regard for the inner requirements of the nature of each, without selecting and screening out that which does not conform to one's expectations or preferences. The ecology movement is a good example, by which one comes to a best acquaintance with nature by respecting her own inter-relationships and balances even if they are not convenient to our needs for mastery and efficiency. When Eros goes into action, it assumes the motivations to appreciate, to care, or to love. Passional involvement and desire are its manner.

One of the striking features of the psychology of cultural develop-ment is that these Logos and Eros principles have not simply operated side by side in equal measure at all times, but that each has had its times of activation and differentiation in history. Myth and ritual have been the means by which they have made themselves known and articulated in the conditions of certain typical historical junctures.

History reveals the ways in which the Logos and Eros principles have been drawn upon to organize the relationships between the members of societies and between the societies and the surrounding world. I have been particularly motivated to trace the development of the bonding principles that have been at work in the formation of the "social organism,"[3] in an evolutionary framework comparable to that of Joseph Needham[4] and Teilhard de Chardin.[5] The psychological modali-ties of such interrelationships vary from era to era, and my interest has been to determine the means by which such changes in modalities have been brought about. The evidence of activation of the psyche in depth in times of profound change demonstrates that the accompanying tur-bulence and upheaval give rise to the occurrence of altered states of consciousness in the form of visionary states in seers and prophets.[6]

In an exploration of the myth and ritual of the dawn of urban culture in various parts of the world,[7] I have attempted to demonstrate that the gods that came into being at that time personified the capacities for mastery and power just newly making themselves felt. Societies were being regimented and economics ordered in ways unknown before; kingdoms became established and firmly structured, empires and colonies were built by new modes of warfare and military organization and conquest. The new figure among the dramatis personae of myth and ritual of various peoples of that time, from five thousand to three thousand years ago, was the storm god,[8] now no longer content to be the fertilizing agent for Mother Earth by inseminating her with his rains; he was now the war god, whose thunder hammer or lightning bolt was his weapon of military mastery and dominance. New dimensions of violence and oppression were making themselves familiar on a prosperous but bloody world stage.

Much attention has been given in recent decades in cultural anthropology to the phenomena of acculturation and rise of "crisis cults" and "revitalization movements"[9] in times of rapid culture change. The great religions of antiquity are thought now to have arisen in the form of crisis cults conceived and led by spiritually gifted seers who experienced the new archetypal forms within their own depths.

The ancient religions best known to us that arose at the dawn of city cultures, the so-called urban revolution,[10] certainly give this impression. For example, in his study of early Egyptian sacral kingship, Frankfort[11] draws the conclusion that myth and ritual forms that rendered the meaning of that kingdom's new social structure and rule were the conception of a visionary genius, who in all likelihood may have been its first pharaoh, Nar-mer or Menes. The constellation of old titanic figures of Horus, Osiris, Seth, and Isis and Nephthys, appeared on the Egyptian national stage in reordered functions de novo and remained dominant for three millennia.

Similarly, in early Israel, most probably David was such a seer and cult founder who gave expression to the needs of his people's new urban culture in the ideology and ceremonial of a sacral monarchy representing the supreme kingship of a transformed Yahweh.[12]

I conclude from this history that the task of the visionary mind at the opening of the urban era was to activate and give full expression to the archetypes of the power principle, which gave so dynamic a motivation to the energetic empire-building of that time.

Within a few centuries, however, in many of those same cultures profound compensatory movements set in to activate and give expression to the opposite Eros principle. The historical material in the ensuing paragraphs I will touch upon only briefly to indicate the manner in which the Eros principle made its appearance in certain cultures of antiquity; it will be narrated in more full detail in chapter 10 in the context of the emergence of individuality in those cultures.

The most dramatically articulate of these took place in China, in the Age of the Hundred Philosophers, the middle of the first millennium B.C.E. In an age of oppression when the people were being bullied by an irresponsible aristocracy of petty kings and nobles, Confucius recommended reforms based upon "human-heartedness."[13] An extensive reexamination of the emotional dynamics of government took place. The authority of the king, the Son of Heaven, was based upon the model of the father. As the son owed allegiance and loyalty to the father in the governing of the family, so on the level of governing the people, subjects owed the same allegiance and loyalty to their prince.[14] This was an explicit psychoanalytic theory 2,500 years before Freud! In the fifth and fourth centuries B.C.E., however, Mo-tse pronounced a doctrine that was an equally explicit Christian theory several centuries before Christ![15] He held that it was not enough for sons to love fathers, or people to love their prince, but that the true welfare of the people depended on the practice of universal love, *chien-ai*. His followers were ardent but uncouth, and went about the courts of the princes of the realm to persuade them to give up arms and bloodshed and adopt a pacifist way of statecraft.[16] One might call them the world's first hippies preaching love and peace and burning draft cards!

Likewise in the middle of the first millennium B.C.E., the Buddhist teaching put the ideology of the sacral kingship, and thus the archetype of the king, through some profoundly significant modification. It taught that at birth it may be recognized that a certain individual is born to greatness, but he has the choice whether to express this in the sacral office of governing as king, or in the corresponding sacred role of becoming an Enlightened One.[17] Both are callings to preeminence over the people, the one in terms of the wise and beneficent uses of power to rule them, the other in terms of universal compassion (Eros), to liberate them from the bonds of attachment and suffering.

I might add that in ancient China, too, there was a similar doctrine that the fully accomplished, "true" man had the option whether to live this state in the role of the Son of Heaven as a ruler, or that of the sage who would instruct the ruler and the people in the "Way of Nature," the Tao.[18]

In our own Judeo-Christian history similar trends took place in the middle of that millennium.[19] The ideal of the kingship as established under David was upheld by the early prophets, reiterating the kingly qualities of righteousness, justice, and peace. During the Exile and after, this became a future hope, that the nation should be saved by a royal servant of the Lord springing from the House of David.[20] Among the anticipated fruits of the reign of such a savior king, a messiah, would be that the people themselves would have the law "written in their inward parts," that is, that autocratic rule over them from a strong political center would become less and less necessary. Although the work of military chastisement of unjust worldly powers would still be carried out by the messianic king, still the ideal of a new era of peace and abundance was proclaimed.[21] In short, what used to be considered a virtue of the good ruler, that he should be strong and accomplished in warfare so as to hold Israel's lead over the nations, now was thrown into a different light and took on the aspect of an unfortunate necessity as a prelude to a reign of peace, where swords would be beaten into plowshares and man would live in harmony with man.

One searches in vain in the Judeo-Christian tradition for any explicit doctrine of love or brotherhood of man until the last couple of centuries before the Christian era. Mercy and compassion began to slip into the enumeration of virtues in late writings like the Book of Enoch.[22] Even more clearly in the Dead Sea Scrolls of the Qumran community the love of the brethren for one another became finally articulated.[23] It remained for the vision of Jesus and of the Apostles to put the principles of love at the center of the qualities of the ideal Davidic and messianic kingship.

In this evolution the sacral king, called "father of the people" and "good shepherd," typically assumed various functions of the earlier tribal clan father, among which were mercy and benevolent protectiveness. For instance, in the Judeo-Christian tradition Yahweh was "Israel's true king," whose "sure mercies" and loving kindness were the earliest model of the later love of the brethren for one another.

In this brief and summary review of the history of the early activation and expression of the Eros principle in various major cultures, two elements stand out. One is that the whole evolution takes place within the framework of the ideology of the sacral kingship. Translated into Jungian psychological formulation, this means that the development of this principle belongs to the archetype of the Center (the "Self").[24]

The other impressive element is that the breakthroughs in the differentiation of the Eros mode of living in society were the work of prophets, seers, mystics, and philosophers. In all, the new capacities were the product of the visionary mind. Visionary states are ones in which the archetypal psyche is activated and has the opportunity to make creative leaps forward in the differentiation and development of its own potentials through its myth-making activity.

The insights of the great mystics have given testimony to this work of the visionary mind in differentiating the Logos and Eros modes of experience. The two outstanding phenomena characterizing the height and apex of the mystical ecstasy are described frequently in Western writing as the overpowering "illumination of the understanding" on the one hand and the overwhelming "rapture of burning love" on the other.[25]

Turning now from the ancient ways of expressing these modes of experience to our most recent framework of them, it has now become generally familiar that the two cerebral hemispheres have their specialized modes of orientation and function. In the work of Ornstein[26] and

Deikman[27] we are given a picture of a left brain geared for an "active" stance in relation to the world for the purposes of a finely articulated mastery, and a right brain for a "receptive" stance for purposes of maximal intake of the data of input. The left side in this case would serve to manipulate and master, the right to relate fully to what is there and take in its whole configuration.

One of the essential observations concerning the right and left brain is that only at the human level of the evolution of primates do these two cerebral hemispheres reveal so marked a specialization of function. I would like to offer the hypothesis that this differentiation is traceable in history. The role of visionary states of the psyche has been to accomplish the explicit functioning of the modes of mastery and power over the environment in one kind of era, and of receptivity and related-ness in another. The archetypal expressions in myth and ritual form, and later in the language of mystical vision, have been the vehicle by which these evolutionary developments were effected in the history of cultures. The human mind cannot be grasped by studies of brain functioning alone, of course, and needs to be explored in the full range of its cultural experience and expression. In this regard I will return to my starting point, the problem of psychosis as a visionary state.

The chief factor determining the difference between the visionary and the "psychotic" experiences may well not be the degree of activation of the lower centers in the high arousal states, as the low and high arousal states are so clearly described by Roland Fischer[28] in his cartog-raphy of ecstatic and meditative states. The attitude of the social milieu toward visionary states is itself apparently the decisive factor in the formation of the symptoms of psychopathology; it is also crucial to the probability that persons caught in the "psychotically" altered states of consciousness will be either regarded as saints or be sent down river in the Ship of Fools, or even be caged as being regressed to the level of beasts.[29] Schizophrenic "psychosis" then becomes more of a cultural problem than a medical one when seen in the perspective of history.

If we can be clear about the central role of visionary states in the forward movement of cultures in their acute crises of change, and knowledgeable about the modes in which the archetypal foundations of experience go about their work of differentiation and specialization, then we will know better what to do with persons who are on their inward journey in the so-called psychotic form.

Differentiating out of a difficult societal milieu is at the same time the effort to establish one's individuality founded upon the self-image. This is a requirement of human nature that appeared only at certain junctures in cultural evolution, to be narrated now.

Chapter 10

Individuality in Myth and Ritual

My intention in this discussion is to trace the rise and gradual evolution of individuality in cultural history. To grasp the import of this development we must first ask what we mean by individuality: one could ask, Isn't everyone an individual, after all? In answer I will start with the simple phrase, "self-determination," implying the accomplishment of one's unique selfhood by fulfilling one's potential capacities in one's own way, thus to reach a state of integration and wholeness. In a traditional culture this is valued differently: in it, one's role is defined by collective agreement and one fulfills one's duties according to one's place in the social structure.

In this historical approach it is, of course, precarious to make general assumptions about cultures, yet in myth and ritual the question of individuality in evolution at each point finds clear representation.

In both the ancient practices and the experiences of persons today, the imagery of a spiritual Center is prominent, one from which order and organization are produced either in the individual psyche or in the society as a whole. It is impressive to observe in these histories how strong an emotional investment there is in honoring and revering the representation of this Center. The emotional tone is consistently a sense of majesty in someone or something, toward which one feels awe. It is in the historical development of the representation of this spiritual Center that we find the clearest evidence of the step-by-step evolution of individuality. This image is, of course, what Jung has called the "archetype of the Self," represented characteristically as a quadripartite circle or mandala that combines, unites, or reconciles the opposites.

I will begin at the juncture in the story of many ancient cultures at which there first appeared the ritual figure of the "Great Man" or "Unique Man" as ruler. This motif occurred in the context of the first appearance of true city cultures in the "urban revolution"[1] occurring in four great river valleys of the Near and Far East, the Nile, the Tigris-Euphrates, the Indus, and the Yellow River, in the third and second millennium B.C.E. The term "city" here signifies a culture newly organized according to function and specialized occupation as against the earlier modes organized according to clan structure.

In these Bronze Age city-states there was a tendency to represent ceremonially the Unique Man as sacral king[2] with divine attributes and to place his function at the cosmic axis or world center, that is, at the midpoint of the world-image. The world was regarded as kingdom, the kingdom as the world. These sacral kings were usually personifications of the Center and of the very life of the kingdom, as its soul, so much that whatever happened to the king happened also to the entire realm. Thus the society was usually regarded as a corporate body with the king as its very heart and soul.

Examples of the sacral kingship in the ancient Near East afford the clearest parallels to the renewal process seen in the visionary states of today, while those in the Far East present the most vivid imagery of the theme of the Center.

The New Year festivals[3] of rejuvenation of the king and the kingdom in the city-states of Mesopotamia follow quite exactly the groundplan of the renewal process that I have outlined already: taking place at the Center, reversing time to the beginning of creation, the symbolic death and rejuvenation of the king, the ritual combat between order and chaos, the reenthronement of the victorious king and his *hieros gamos* or sacred marriage, and the reading of the destinies as a reaffirmation of the will of the gods and of the society's allegiance to it. The temple's stage tower represented a world mountain and cosmic axis called *Dur Anki*, the Bond of Heaven and Earth, and was the locus of the king's death and renewal ritually. In the early Sumerian years the king was called *Lugal*, the Great Man, playing the role of the god of the high sky as the upholder of order, and that of the storm god as warrior and chief executive.

Egypt's festivals of reenthronement followed roughly the same pattern, but its kingship was noteworthy for the absolute divinity of the pharaoh: he was Horus, god of light of the sky, and Horus was the pharaoh, in the early dynasties. As Giver of Life and Giver of Order, his *ka* or soul provided the *kas* for all his subjects, who thereby participated in his life as he did in theirs. As this source of life, order, and well-being for the realm, the king's position in the scheme of things was at the Center, his throne set upon the primordial mound representing the spot of land from which the whole creation spread out into the four directions. His capital city, Memphis, was set at the midpoint of the Egyptian world between the two lands, Upper and Lower Egypt. The kingship was dual also in another sense; as Horus, the pharaoh ruled the realm of the living, while the recently deceased king was transfigured into Osiris, who then reigned over the realm of the dead, the ancestors.

India, too, though in much later centuries, had its sacral kingship in which the monarch's person was regarded as a composite of eight divinities; as Chakravartin, Wheel King, his rule was viewed as universal. The *rajasuya* rites of enthronement and reenthronement emphasized centrality and also rebirth, vividly and explicity dramatized by his assumption of the cowl of the chorion and of the amnion, and of the waters of the amniotic fluid of the fetal state.

Among the ceremonial expressions of sovereignty in the ancient world, that of the Chinese is outstandingly satisfying both spiritually and a esthetically. Its cosmological setting is a source of delight to modern evolutionists with a systems theory approach such as Joseph Needham,[4] who said of it that there was no belief in a creator acting from outside, but that this cosmos was a "self-contained, self-organizing system." In these purely naturalistic terms "the harmonious cooperation of all beings arose, not from the orders of a superior authority external to themselves, but from the fact that they were all parts in a hierarchy of wholes forming a cosmic pattern, and what they obeyed were the internal dictates of their own natures." This was the model upon which the manner of governing in the earliest dynasties was founded. "Heaven" was a barely personified presence presiding over the cosmos, and the "Son of Heaven" was sovereign but did not actively rule this confederacy of principalities.

This Heaven was in the Bronze Age regarded as made up of the spirits of the departed royal ancestors, the *ti*,[5] acting as a composite whole; only the sacral king possessed a soul that would become immortalized as such a *ti*. The ideogram for *ti* was a vertical phallus, suggesting the generative, life-giving function of such ancestral spirits, not unlike the role of Osiris in Egypt.

The theme of the Great Individual was suffused throughout this ideology of the kingship.[6] Heaven, *T'ien*, was in its earliest written form represented by the character in figure 10.1, obviously signifying the Great Man, that is, the conglomerate embodiment of the *ti*. It is now written as in figure 2. In the second dynasty (first millennium B.C.E.), the Chou, we find the sacral king represented by the character in figure 3, the Great Man now with his feet planted on the ground. He was *T'ien-tse*, the Son of Heaven, and participated in the nature of Heaven itself, as spokesman and mediator. This meant that the accumulated experience of the ancestors was embodied in the sacral king. The Son of Heaven alone, as the ruling member of the dynasty, could assume the title of *Wang*, the king, as his special prerogative. It is written as in figure 4, representing, according to later philosophers,[7] a cosmic axis with Heaven, Man, and Earth united through the person of the king, a beautiful rendering of the role of the Center.

FIGURE 10.1

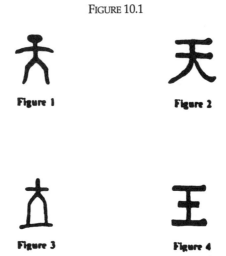

Figure 1   Figure 2

Figure 3   Figure 4

Figure 5

Among the many indications of the central position of this sacred figure, there is a consistent emphasis on its being not only a midpoint but also a north-south axis. The name of China is written in characters implying this, as seen in figure 5: *Chung Kuo*, the "Middle Kingdom," with "center" as a rectangle traversed by a vertical line or an axis, and "kingdom" as a square enclosure containing lines indicative of the kingship.

FIGURE 10.2

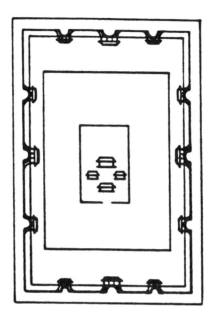

The capital cities of the Shang and Chou dynasties[8] (second and first millennia B.C.E.) were laid out in the manner represented in figure 10.2. Each was a quadripartite (square or rectangular) city with avenues and gates oriented to the cardinal directions, and in the center the king's palace faced south on an axis dividing the populace into two halves, according to lineage. In front of the palace on one side was the Temple of the Ancestors, important to the function of mediator, and on the other side the Altar of Earth, concerned with the feminine principle of increase and life-giving. There is here, then, a Yang and Yin, a Heaven and Earth, division in these two sacred places, temple and altar, on either side of the axis.

A little later on, the kingdom that is the earth, that is, the ordered world, was represented in the bronze cosmic mirrors of the Han dynasty (the end of the first millennium B.C.E.), as seen in figure 10.3, called the TLV design.[9] The Middle Kingdom was seen as a square with gates in the cardinal directions (the Ts), and marks near the periphery of the design (the Vs) indicating that there is an implied cross here with limbs extending out, and with the Ls suggesting a swastika perhaps. These areas (the "Four Seas") in the four directions were considered the realms of the barbarians, that is, of the chaos that was the king's task to bring

FIGURE 10.3

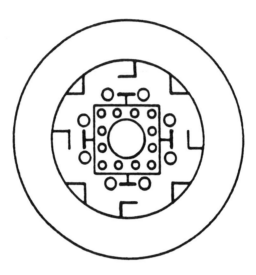

into the organization of the ordered world as his cosmocratic function, the creation being viewed as an ongoing process. The Son of Heaven had his position at the center of the bronze mirror, indicated by a burnished boss.

Also, in the dimension of actuality, the kingdom had roughly the shape of an encircled square, more or less, with the four sacred mountains in the cardinal directions and a fifth at the center, which had a certain ritual significance at that time. The centrality, the quadrating of space, and the strict ordering and balancing of design were thoroughly represented in these symbolic forms. These mandala patterns antedated the Tibetan ones by many centuries.

A very interesting further representation of centrality was the ceremonial building for the function of the king, which was the *Ming T'ang*, the "Hall of Light" or "Hall of Brilliance," where he performed his kingly rituals[10] (figure 10.4). It was "square below" representing earth, and "round above" representing the dome of the sky; here he would observe the night heavens and keep track of time and the seasons. It was all surrounded by a *pi* moat, which signified Heaven again. In the central building was an audience hall where the Son of Heaven would sit on his throne with the pole star at his back, facing the south. This was surrounded by four square chapels in early times, later by eight, and upstairs was the round observatory platform. The kings of very early

FIGURE 10.4

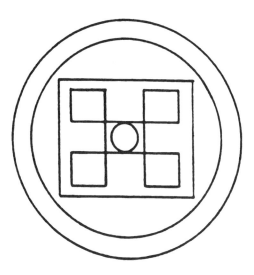

times had had the custom of making the ceremonial rounds of the entire kingdom by going to the five holy mountains, not to explore, but to confirm his active relation to the four quarters of the realm and, as they put it, "to spread his virtue among them." It was not too long before they considered that a bit wearisome and instead they traveled only to the four gates of the capital city. Finally they did all this in the Ming-T'ang alone, making the rounds of the four quarters and also of the seasons and the months. This was considered to be the function of the king as "master of time" and "master of space." He faced the south with the pole star at his back, toward which the stars of heaven would turn and would circulate around it. This was the function of the sacral king: like the pole star, the people would turn their gaze upon him and the life of the realm would circulate about him, so to speak, and thus "remain calm and docile," in harmony.

Scholars have brought to light recently that these kings of the Shang and the early Chou dynasty were also considered shamans.[11] They have been known as "rain kings" for some time, but that was the least of their functions. They also had the ability to fly like shamans into the heavens, and they could traverse earth, water, and air at will. They had powers of divination and prognostication and they apparently had healing powers as well. The Shang bronzes that have become generally familiar and have been unearthed during the past century, show animals sculpted around them, facing each other in pairs. There have been studies of such animals in the past few years, and it has been found that these are the helping animals of the shaman, those who give him his shamanic powers. Therefore, to have big cauldrons made of bronze, made so exquisitely with many animals around them, was a designation of the spiritually effective powers of such a sacral king.

The monarch was also a father figure: he had a benevolent role, caring for the people with concern for their welfare, like Heaven, and he carried the responsibility for the well-being of the people.

The sage kings of antiquity—of the legendary first dynasty, the Hsia dynasty of the latter third millennium B.C.E.—were exemplars of this particular kind of virtue, of responsibility, of caring, and of nonassertion, *wu-wei*, governing without asserting heavy-handed or authoritarian dominance.

There is something about this mythic psychology that is always evanescent, and evolution moves relentlessly forward. All this ceremonial system became desanctified very soon. For it to be sacred or sanctified means that an archetypal conviction or dynamic suffused it. The kingship was then filled with potential for the future. It was a psychologically pregnant state about to give birth to many particular attributes of consciousness that would follow in the succeeding centuries but that at first were represented merely in symbolic form or in ritual ceremonial. The myth and ritual were essential to provide the new meaning for the new lifestyle of this kind of urban society. The habit throughout history is that myth arises in times of bewilderment among changing conditions and offers the necessary guidelines for psychic energies in innovative culture forms. Then gradually the personifications or representations of those images become desanctified and secularized.

The fate of this mode of governance was most clearly expressed in the histories of Egypt and of China.[12] In both of these, the prerogatives and privileges of royalty were increasingly mimicked by the aristocracy. Petty princes and rulers of the component states composing the realm took upon themselves these attributes as they governed more and more autonomously, built equally magnificent palaces and tombs for themselves, and gathered large armies to assert their governing power. In this way the sacred potency and prestige of the status of the "Great Individual" gradually diffused out from the Center and became more and more secularized. Ambition and greed for expanding land and mounting wealth led to unceasing warring of these nobles against one another.

The Egyptian experience is noteworthy in a number of respects. In their feudal age in the latter part of the third millennium B.C.E. appeared a kind of prophetism[13] that was to recur in Israel almost two thousand years later in the same mode. Wise men like Ipuwer lamented the lawlessness, marauding, and prevailing poverty and laid the blame for this chaos squarely on the pharaoh for not carrying out the duties of his function, introducing then the vision of a messianic hero who would restore the virtues of the ideal of the kingship. Another significant development was the democratization of the role of Osiris in the mortuary cult.

In the early dynasties the king alone had the privilege of being transfigured into Osiris as King of the Dead; soon the aristocracy, instead of merely accompanying the monarch on his journey after death, began to assume the right to be similarly transformed into the Osirian status, and finally the common man could by the same funerary procedure "become an Osiris" at his death. These phenomena portray graphically the diffusion of the attributes of the Center downward and outward to the members of the society.

In China much the same sort of history occurred, but two thousand years later.[14] The Chou dynasty during the first half of the first millennium B.C.E. gradually lost its authority in all but name, and a feudal age followed in which the parts strove against each other at the expense of the welfare of the whole. Times of dire distress and intense suffering among the people resulted from their being ground down as crops and manpower were appropriated for the warring armies of the various states in their power struggles against one another. However, in China's "time of troubles," in the midst of her most critical years when the culture's very survival was seriously threatened, a remarkable phenomenon took place.

A strong move toward healing was undertaken by gifted visionaries, that is, by the "Hundred Schools" of the philosophers, consisting of efforts to reexamine the basic principles of governance and of societal cohesion by spiritual cultivation. I will summarize these briefly by highlighting certain of their doctrines.

In spite of the public image of Confucius as an advocate of a sort of Victorian propriety, he was in fact one of the great revolutionaries of history, championing a new concept of democracy. He advocated a new principle possessing a mystique comparable to that of the Tao among the Quietists: this was a virtue (i.e., a force) called *jen*, meaning a human-heartedness, compassion, or loving caring. Under its influence the society would function as one great family in which all men would be brothers; this was the original implication of "brotherly love." When asked about perfect knowledge, he said it was "to know all men," and about perfect virtue, he said it was "to love all men."[15] He also originated the concept of the Golden Rule, and of the equality of all men including even the "barbarians," an idea too preposterous to be acceptable at the time.

A century later the foremost follower of Confucius, Mencius,[16] taught that selflessness can lead one to an identification of the self with the universe to such an extent that one may realize that the myriad things of the cosmos are all within us. By such spiritual cultivation all men are capable of becoming sage-kings like the great exemplars of the kingship, Yao and Shun. He was a perceptive psychologist who traced the origins of the dynamics of societal relationships between rulers and ruled to those within the family system between parents and children. Goodness, he said, was innate.

An opponent of the Confucian school was Mo-tse,[17] who proclaimed a doctrine of universal love, *chien ai*, a virtue (i.e., a force) to be developed by spiritual cultivation: he argued that the model of the family was not universal enough, and that all men should hold an equal love for one another. He was a pre-Christian Christian.

The Taoists[18] were also opponents of the Confucian teachings, declaring that those scholars talked too much and that the more one talks of virtues of love and loyalty and benevolence, the more one betrays the fact that one does not yet have them. If one follows the Way of Nature, one does not need such admonitions. By cultivating the light the spiritual Center is found inside, not needing a representation in the center of government.

My conclusion, then, is that these doctrines reveal the insight that the societal harmony that had once emanated from the benevolence generated by the Son of Heaven at the center of the world now was to be cultivated from within the individuals composing the society. The Center of order and integration, once put out into external expression in the myth and ritual of the kingship, was now found inside. Order need not be imposed from above if it is evoked from within. In this I find a remarkable parallel once more to the visionary experience that has been called "psychotic"; this typically starts with imagery of power and dominance, and with concerns of inordinate prestige, but ends with equally compelling concerns for capacities for loving relationship in the lives of both the individual and the society.

This level of spiritual sophistication and insight was not reached by most cultures of the ancient Near East, which spent their energies in warring one against the other: Sumer disappeared as mysteriously as it had arrived; Akkad, which, overran Sumer, was in its turn taken over by the Assyrians, until both merged in the empire of Cyrus of Iran. None had a chance to reach full cultural maturity as did China, and it was left to Israel to accomplish the task of inward realization and internalization of the kingship.

In Israel, as is well known, many centuries of visionary work by its prophets began with the desire for the restoration of the ideal of the sacral kingship in a strong ruler, but evolved into a more subtle concept of a messiah who would be a spiritual shepherd of the people. Jesus brought the various elements of this long tradition into a refined expression of a purely inward and nonpolitical image of his Davidic kingship characterized by an ethic of *agapē*, a love of all the members of this kingdom of God for one another.

In India, too, Gautama Buddha had the choice whether to follow the career of a *charkravartin*, a universal king, for which he was born and raised, or that of an Enlightened One, for which he prepared himself by his meditation under the Bo tree. He, too, of course, advocated a way of life characterized by compassion and kindliness toward all beings. Both this Buddhahood and this Christ-nature represent the perfected form of the inner sacral kingship as a psychic reality.

To recapitulate briefly this evolutionary development, at the beginning of the urban revolution, the spiritual Center was first projected out in externalized form in the figure of the sole Great Individual, the sacral king. As it gradually diffused out among the members of the aristocracy, this individuality became secularized and desanctified to the point of becoming a willful self-seeking. Under the duress of the crisis as the societies became increasingly chaotic, prophets and visionaries proclaimed the vision of the inward realization of the Center and its kingly myth and ritual forms. This internalization marked the beginning of the full democratization of these forms, which then should be regarded as the true meaning of democracy. It raised the need for a new principle in which order might be preserved in societal structures, and for this the visionaries perceived the dynamic of loving fellowship and compassion as an absolute prerequisite to make the new individuality work. It was seen as the necessary counterbalance to the motives of personal power, which otherwise only led to social chaos.

This history demonstrates then that this species of individuality is safe and healthy for society only if it is kept in balance with societal concern, and if personal power motivations are compensated by those of caring for persons.

Needless to say, the problems we are facing today in our new style of urban life grow out of an individuality that has become a mere self-seeking, and a democracy that has lost the heart of its meaning. In America, especially, individuals live as if in separateness or even isolation. In a competitive system one is out for oneself. The parts once more seem to be functioning without regard for the interests of the whole.

Immense numbers of persons grow up without belonging to community and hence without incentives to loyalty; crime, visible and invisible, mounts.

When individuality has not developed in the way needed for harmonious social articulation, or when it has taken a wrong turn and one finds oneself out of tune with one's world, there is need for healing either from one's self-organizing processes or from external sources. If we look over the various myth and ritual practices of healing in various ages and parts of the world, we find both the inner and the outer ways to follow the same configuration.

Chapter 11

Healing in Myth and Ritual

The patterns of healing ceremonial seem surprisingly widespread. In the early 1970s I was invited on several occasions to be consultant to a newly established psychiatric facility for the Navaho reservation, the dates being carefully designed to coincide with Native American ceremonials. It was, of course, a great delight to me to have this privilege of attending rituals that were free of the self-consciousness marking the more popular ones that were overrun by tourists, but one of them held a surprise that left a deep impression on me.

Hastily painted signs on cardboard pointed the turns and roads across the prairie to this "Fire Dance," more precisely known as "Mountain Way." It was night and cold, and the ground was snow-covered as we entered the immense "Circle of Boughs" through its opening on the east. A throng of a thousand or more were standing clustered around small fires, members of clan and neighborhood, all assembled here to participate in the healing process of a young woman patient; she was in the eight-sided hogan over on the other side, seated on a sand-painting and surrounded by a group of chanters and the medicine man. Now an impressive cone of upright cedar trunks was sending its flames leaping up toward the starry sky and lighting up the faces all around. Hour by hour through the night the troupe of dancers circled around the central fire. First, they carried little flaming sticks portraying the element fire; second graceful lattices of feathers representing air; then a vessel for the element water; finally a plant was made to bloom as a representation of the wondrously life-giving powers of the earth. The songs accompanying the dances told of the stages of creation, characterized by these four elements representing the four levels ascended by the first beings, from the lowest underworld up to the present world, as narrated in the emergence myth. It was typical, I was told, for Navaho healing rituals to reenact creation; to be ill was to be out of tune with the world, and the cure was then to put the patient back to the beginnings of time and so to experience the creation of the world and establish the right relation to it.[1]

One minor consequence of this experience was my taking the account of this ceremonial to the staff of the Agnew Project, our experimental study of the treatment of acute "psychosis" with and without medication. I was struck by the contrast between the picture of a healing process in the midst of a participating neighborhood community, all involved in the procedures, and that other picture of hospital wards where patients were all too often left to their own devices while the medication did the work. The staff seized upon the concept and devised a "vigil" in a specially designed room with constant attendance upon a single patient, for a few days, by a couple, a man and a woman, for each eight-hour shift to encourage going down into the ultimate depths of the psychic process, encouraging regression to mother, breast, and even the womb. However, that is not the story I intend to dwell upon.

What excited me far more profoundly was the content of this myth and ritual process enacted as a healing, because for twenty years I had been observing this creation motif in persons undergoing "psychotic" visionary states as a major element in their self-healing. I had been finding this "return to the beginnings" to have two concurrent aspects: a regression to childhood, infancy, or the womb, moving hand in hand with the return to Eden and the beginnings of time, even to the chaos before it, frequently accompanied by imagery of the final Armageddon and world destruction. I will briefly narrate a few of the more colorful examples (1949–61):[2]

A young male: He was in the Garden of Eden as Adam with his female psychiatrist as Eve, with David as their son. "The Garden of Eden will live forever!" he exclaimed. Hell took over Eden from Adam, Eve, and Christ, the four being depicted as a cross in a circle. "The War of the Kings will be the end," those of the north, east, south, and west; he as hero would prevent this and stop the Communists from blowing up the world.

A young male: Time for him was going backward, represented in diagramatic form as a clock with the sun at the center and the quarter-hours as the four cardinal directions, but in reverse. His task was to save the world from destruction in the war between Communism and Catholicism.

A young woman: Her task was to go back to the beginnings of creation and to repeat it all from the start, and to go through the whole process of evolution step by step. She saw it in the primordial sea with its monsters, then on land with its reptiles, and later among the primitives with their rituals. At the same time she had to return similarly to her own birth and repeat the stages of her growth up to the present, but without error, thus having to do it all over if she made a fault. The Devil was trying to destroy the world with radioactive substances and Christ was opposing him to save it, all in the form of the conflict between Communism and Christianity.

A young woman: She had visions of the time of creation and early evolution, seeing the first primitive peoples migrating across the continents and British Isles and Channel. She felt like a little girl. The world was divided in a power struggle between Communism and Democracy. The Bay Area was to go through a cataclysm in which it would drop amid fire and flood to become a New Hell, while San Francisco would become a New Bethlehem, a new heavenly city like the New Jerusalem.

A young woman: For her all the people had died save three women and one man. She found herself in the Garden of Eden as Mother Eve, and this was the beginning of creation; she expected everyone to be "going around as primitives, all naked." Time stood still; her watch was frozen as solid gold. She was returning to the state of a young girl. She was also a divine creatrix, creating three stars and the moon, and peopling them. She felt herself to be the whole universe, as she was fashioning worlds and peopling them. She was expecting an invasion from the Communists.

A young woman: She knew herself to be Eve the temptress, returning to the primitive emotions and ways of the Garden of Eden at the beginning of the world. She also saw the world turning inside-out, so that which had been hidden was now out in the open. Battle lines were drawn up of the struggle of Communism against Christianity, representing Evil against the Good.

So regularly were these themes occurring that one might wonder whether in some way I was influencing them. I can only comment that no one was more surprised than I to hear these visions, and that I had in those years no knowledge of the mythic background behind the imagery in "psychotic" episodes. Only after six years of this work did I learn of the myth and ritual parallels that I will recount.

I was deeply grateful when I found Mircea Eliade's profound study of such motifs in his book, *The Myth of the Eternal Return*,[3] in which, at last, I could recognize the myth-and-ritual parallels to what I had been observing. For here, in the context of a scrutiny of the qualities of time as they are experienced in different cultural levels from the primitive to the sophisticated, he outlined the program of the New Year Festivals of the earliest urban civilizations of the Near East for the renewal of sacral kings and their kingdoms annually. In these rites the main features that I will select and briefly name are the same as in the visions of the "psychotic" persons just quoted:[4]

> The world center is established as a transformative locus; in it a symbolic death occurs; time returns to the beginnings and the world reverts to chaos and is regenerated; a cosmic combat is enacted between the powers of light and darkness or of order and disorder.

That these rites concerned the order of governments and their ruling figures struck me, and seemed to throw light on the question of why in their "psychotic" visions persons seemed to be fully as occupied with issues of political ideologies as with those of their own personal emotional life.

Now, however, I want to deal with the question, why the motif of the return to the beginnings is widely prevalent in processes of healing rites and self-healing visionary states. How are we to understand the function of this retrogression to the starting point?

As Eliade[5] saw it, the key to the question lies in the perception of the nature of time. Archaic societies found meaning and a sense of reality only in actions established by the first ancestral heroes in the "time of origins"; all other actions not so prescribed lacked this sanctification. Time for these peoples was circular and in the cycle of the year all random and profane actions accumulated to the point of a contamination of the world, that is, the culture, comparable to the piling up of sin. Thus it was felt necessary at the end of each annual cycle to rejuvenate the world in ceremonial as a veritable purification. For those societies *"life cannot be repaired*, it can only be *re-created* by a return to sources. And the 'source of sources' is the prodigious outpouring of energy, life and fecundity that occurred at the Creation of the World."[6]

In the ritual expression of this return, sacred space was established, designated as the Center of the world, and so was sacred time, designated as that of the beginnings, both set apart distinctly from profane space and time. Living in cyclic time in which deviations from the archetypal models were given no value, the status of reality was granted only to what conformed to the myths of origins and not to human history: such cultures were nonhistorical. With the cataclysmic changes brought about by the urban revolution of the Bronze Age,[7] for a few centuries the sacral kings were considered identical with the founding gods and heroes of myth, and reality was still defined by myth. As the sense of the onward flow of historical time began to prevail, however, so did the desanctification of the kingship and of the tradition-bound order of society.

In a book written two decades later, *Myth and Reality*,[8] Eliade went over the same ground but with an extended perspective on the ritual return to the beginnings. In the review of a large number of instances of this practice in archaic societies, he stressed the point that any creative act tended to require that the myth of creation be invoked; innovations could in this way be made acceptable as part of reality or could be charged with creative energy. An example is childbirth:

> When a child is born among the Osages, a man who had talked with the gods is summoned. . . . He recites the history of the creation of the Universe and the terrestrial animals to the newborn infant. Not until this has been done is the baby given the breast. Later, when he wants to drink water [he] is called in again. Once again he recites the Creation, ending with the origin of Water. When the child is old enough to eat solid food . . . [he] comes once more and again recites the creation, this time also relating the origin of grains and other foods.[9]

Eliade's impression of the sense of such rites was that the moment of creation of the world was considered a "strong time," charged with tremendous power and that ritual time, being identical to that moment, would share in its creative dynamic. This line of thought led him to the conclusion that the healing rituals of archaic societies were founded on these beliefs in a supercharge of energy drawn from the creation:[10]

> There were many applications of the Polynesian cosmogonic myth, especially healing. It goes as follows:
>
> In the beginning there were only the Waters and Darkness. Io the Supreme God, separated the waters by the power of thought and of his words, and created the Sky and Earth.
>
> He said: "Let the waters be separated, let the Heavens be formed, Let the earth be. . . . These are creative words, charged with sacred power." They are repeated during the rite for making a sterile womb fertile, or for curing the body and mind, or for death, or for war. . . . "The words by which Io caused light to shine in the darkness are used in rituals for cheering a gloomy and despondent

heart, the feeble aged, the decrepit . . . [things], affecting man to despair in times of adverse war."

A fine example of such healing rites is found among the Bhils, an Indo-Tibetan people:

> The magician "purifies" the space beside the patient's bed and draws a *mandol* with corn flour . . . until the patient is completely cured. . . . But the *mandala* is primarily an *imago-mundi*; it represents the cosmos in nature. . . . Its construction is equivalent to a magical re-creation of the world. Hence when the Bhil magician draws a *mandol* . . . he is repeating the cosmogony. . . . The operation certainly has a therapeutic purpose. Made symbolically contempory with the Creation of the World, the patient is immersed in the primordial fullness of life; he is penetrated by gigantic forces that, *in illo tempore*, make the Creation possible."[11]

If among the "psychotic" visions of today, we take the concept of the supercharge of creative energy as a guide to the meaning of the return to the beginnings, I find that it doesn't quite fit. Granted that, with the veritable explosion of highly charged myth-making, the activation of all these archetypes is attended by an energy that altogether overwhelms the ego, still the purpose of the creation motif does not seem to be that. Rather, what we are told by persons having these visions is that they return to creation in order to start over again from the very first fashioning of the world, and to repeat the entire evolutionary development that followed, hand in hand with a review of one's own personal history since birth. This reenactment of one's life appears to be intended by nature as its precious gift of an opportunity to relive those early years in order to right the wrongs that had occurred, to heal the hurts and disentangle the distortions of the early development of the self.

In these visions the frequent allusions to the sight of peoples of the earliest times migrating to their various continents seem to refer to early phases of the development of consciousness. The standpoint of the ideation is modern, within an evolutionary framework of a cultural level that has a sense of history, where time is not circular but linear, where history is not static but changing, and where the person is no longer entrapped in custom but struggles to emerge out of the collectivity into true individuality.

In reviewing these practices of healing and self-healing, it has become evident that the psyche reaches for cure by reviewing and reenacting its past, its ultimate past to the beginning of its evolution. This may answer a question that might well have been on the mind of the reader: Why has so much attention been devoted to the history of myth and ritual in this chapter and the last two? The gradual differentiation of the Logos and Eros modes and of individuality were accomplished in cultural forms after being imaged first in visionary experience and then in myth and ritual expression. Here we must remind ourselves that in all the stepwise evolution of organisms it is recognized that in each single one the *entire* past of its species is repeated, and thus ontogeny recapitulates phylogeny. The psychic aspect of the human organism is no exception. The visionary images of the creation and development of races are a vivid manifestation of this very recapitulation. If a well-endowed psyche is going to differentiate its various aptitudes and functions to grow into its wholeness, it must undergo that step-by-step progress from the beginning point toward bringing it all into consciousness. Usually it happens autonomously on an unconscious level, but in procedures such as dream work or in visionary experience it comes to conscious recognition.

Another element in the "psychotic" visions is rich in meaning: accompanying the creation theme is the image of political parties in conflict, having parallels in the motif of the cosmic combat in ancient rituals. Here let me point again to the tremendous stress upon concerns of social and religious reform and the urgent call to save the world from destruction by evil forces, all outweighing the more personal trials of one's own emotional development. One gets the impression of a great supercharge of energy in the feelings of messianic calling on the world stage. In my puzzlement over the great predominance of this motif in the visions I found the work of Wallace and of Lanternari to be most illuminating.

Wallace[12] made an important contribution in his formulation of the distressing turmoils of acculturation, when societies tend to disintegrate under the impact of cultures of higher-level complexity, but are reconstructed by " revitalization movements" initiated by prophets. In their psychosis-like "paranoid hallucinations," as he calls them, these seers are overwhelmed with visions of the end of the world and of journeys into the heavens, and from these they provide their societies with new myths and cults around which the societies reorganize. Lanternari[13] similarly made extensive studies of new religions in cultures oppressed by colonialist intrusion and dominance; in a large sample of such movements he found regularities in the program of prophetic visions and in the resulting cultic myth and ceremonial (see note 8 in chapter 3).

An example of the motif of world regeneration is the prophetic vision of an Amerindian, a Paiute living a century ago in the territory now at the border of California and Nevada:

On a mountainside he beheld the world opening up a huge chasm and totally collapsing into it (an alternate account said it rolled up like a carpet). For days nothing and no one existed, but on the third day the world was recreated anew, now as a paradise in which the Native Americans dwelt in the company of their deceased ancestors and the Great Spirit himself. No white people were granted the privilege of sharing this happy land, yet their much-coveted implements were there for the use of all present![14]

This revelation gave rise to the famous Ghost Dance to dramatize and reenact it, a ceremony that spread rapidly from coast to coast among numerous tribes as an expression of their desperate hope for survival in the new conditions of white dominance.

One could cite many instances of native American prophetic visions: Handsome Lake of the Iroquois, Black Elk of the Sioux, John Wilson and his influence on the Native American Church, and many more.

In India, Fuchs has made an investigation of messianic movements and found a common sequence of motifs that echoed the ones we are enumerating here. When discontent with a society's condition reaches a certain pitch, the prevalence of hysterical symptoms rises and the people turn to drugs and alcohol. A visionary figure gathers a following and starts a cult demanding absolute faith and obedience; he orders them to change their lifestyle and destroy their property. He issues a call to revolt against the ruling authority and makes moves to restore the traditional culture-forms, engendering a myth promising a renewal of the world beginning with a catastrophe and ending with the establishment of an earthly paradise and a new golden age. As with the Native Americans, the desired material goods of the alien dominant culture are granted to the renewed society.

Prophetic and messianic visions occurring all over the world thus show in their image sequences remarkable similarities to one another and to the "psychotic" visions of today, and in all these the theme of world destruction and regeneration occurs with considerable consistency. To me this suggests that the psychic healing process with its regular mythic structure does its work in two principal areas: on one side there is self-healing in the individual person's renewal process, and on the other, cultural healing in the visionary work of the prophet. In both areas the formation of a new world-image lies at the heart of the process.

Another source of visionary image-sequences conforming to this model is the near-death experiences that Kenneth Ring has studied and formulated.[15] In episodes of brief clinical death he has observed prophetic visions of the end of the world, in which great cataclysms of destruction lead over into its transformation into a new age of peace and brotherhood.[16] In a recent article he has come to the conclusion that such glimpses into a near future are best taken as symbolic renderings of psychic changes in world-image rather than as future events. It is a timely comment, especially since the prophecies generally pointed to the year 1988 for the crisis! I am tempted to think that the present collective world-image might be in process of change this year, from one split into two halves hostile to each other and toward one that is beginning to loosen this frozen opposition, and allow a modicum of peaceable interchange.

Still another source of such image-sequences is one that contrasts with the role of prophets, who are motivated by their strong sense of responsibility for the welfare of their people and reform of their culture. From Jung's painstaking research into the visionary work of the Nature philosophers of the late medieval and Renaissance eras,[17] one gets the impression of solitaries working in seclusion intensively in their alchemical laboratories on procedures that were somewhat secret because of the dangers of promoting their highly heretical doctrines. The adepts' efforts were dedicated to exploring new views of the nature of matter, on one hand as chemistry and on the other as a vehicle for spiritual processes: the procedures were revealed to them in visions and led to a fresh realization of nature's transformative principle. These discoveries were often quite shaking when they led into a return to the "horrible darkness" of the primordial chaos attended by dread and onsets of depression, in turn giving rise to bright visions of the Creation reenacted in their substances.[18] From these procedures were produced elixirs called *medicina athanasiou* and *pharmacon athanasiou*—medicine and drug of immortality—with healing properties. Not sharing the prophets' urge to advocate publicly their new worldview and ethic, or change their society with new cult forms, the alchemists tended to maintain the stance of practicing the occult

In China's history there are clear expressions of the value of "returning to the root," that is, the origins.[19] The Way of Nature was extolled as the source of the well-being of the world, of society, and of the individual. The Tao operates by constantly reverting back to the beginnings, to the primordial void and the earliest forms of societal life;

in meditation one reverts in this same manner not only to the void but to the "womb breathing" of one's earliest life, and thus to the openly receptive and allowing state of mind in the infant. In this way the king fulfills his function best if he does not govern actively but gives his attention entirely to his own relation to the Tao in sagely quietude. In this Chinese frame of thought, time retains its cyclic quality in the alternating ascent and descent of the virtues endowed by Heaven in the ongoing process of creation. History takes on a somewhat negative cast by the accumulation of profane innovations in the ways of managing society; those ways were errors that could be set right by a constant returning to the experience of the void at the beginning of time and to the innocence of the earliest societies, thus to keep starting afresh in renewed attunement to the Tao.

I want to turn now to the work of one more person wrestling with this question of the healing capabilities of undoing time-consciousness. In his book *Space, Time and Medicine*, Larry Dossey[20] gives an account of a discovery in his medical practice: patients could find their way to self-healing by freeing themselves from the tyranny of the flow of linear time. He argues that brain physiology itself can be changed by mental states to the extent that pain perception may be altered; "pain, an inward index of health, is tied to the time sense in our consciousness."[21] All the current relaxation techniques can be seen, in his view, as aiming to do this work of "invoking a specific psychological mode with regard to time perception."[22] The vivid experience of a nonflowing time can work for health as the exact counterpart of our ability "to destroy ourselves through the creation of illness by perceiving time in a linear, one-way flow";[23] especially, of course, is this the devastating effect of pressured time (as for instance in the well-known cardiac Type A personalities). The ultimate meaning of health and disease, he feels, can only be comprehended through a view in which the definitions of time, space, and matter are aligned with those of modern physics.

Dossey's discussion of these definitions in the new sciences proceeds to make such an alignment, reviewing the salient features in the work of the many pioneers whose names are familiar to those in the transpersonal arena. Among these scientists I wish to point out a few that pertain especially to this investigation of the overhauling of world-view and world-image by means of a return to chaos and the beginnings. In Prigogine's theory of dissipative structures,[24] order is seen to arise out of chaos, and even has to; such structures can be seen to operate at all levels in nature from the microscopic to the social and cultural, a view thoroughly worked out by Erich Jantsch.[25] One of the formulations is that perturbations in the ordinary flux of all living forms may reach such proportions as to allow an escape into higher levels of complexity, and on this point Ferguson makes a cogent comment bearing on worldviews:

> At first the idea of creating a new order by perturbation seems outrageous, like shaking up a box of words and pouring out a sentence. . . . We know that stress often forces suddenly new solutions; that crisis often alerts us to opportunity; that creative process requires chaos before form emerges; that individuals are often strengthened by suffering and conflict.[26]

In this glance at the new style of consciousness in the sciences, Dossey creates a considerable perturbation on his own part in the statement that the space-time view of health and disease recommended for good therapy "tells us that a vital part of the goal of every therapist is to help the sick person toward a reordering of his world-view," recognizing himself as a "process in space-time related to all other phenomena in the universe in an all-embracing oneness, not an isolated entity . . . adrift in flowing time."[27]

Nor is the mythic mode any stranger to the scientific thought of today. Niels Bohr is quoted in this same general context of the bewildering challenges to researchers when their experimental data and their mathematics indicate baffling and paradoxical connections that defy any common sense and any expression in ordinary language. On this Niels Bohr[28] says that "when it comes to atoms, language can be used only as in poetry. . . . Quantum theory . . . provides us with a striking illustration of the fact that we can fully understand a connection though we can only speak of it in images and parables." He adds, "The hallmark of modern science is that it has outrun common sense . . . and run headlong into our metaphorical, poetic self, and some part of our self that mythologizes."

In the field of therapy of all kinds, from technological medicine to the psychotherapies, we have a good deal to learn from Taoism. This doctrine's mode of being in the world, its way of life and its ethic, based as they are on a constant return to the beginnings,[29] have as their natural expression nature's own mode, which is *wu-wei*, that is, a species of action that does not force effects but allows them. This receptive principle permits one to sustain a clear realism because it allows one to see things as they actually are, rather than as one might prefer them to be according to one's own will. Our Western medical stance of forcing change to correct the accidents of disease by active interventions exacts a price: the loss of the fundamental guidelines of the older medicine, the intent to respect and cooperate with the *vis mediatrix naturae*, the healing power of nature. Chinese traditional medicine goes about it differently, helping to improve the entire state of the person by balancing the energies whose deviations have allowed the occurrence of the disease.

To reach an attunement to nature's own way of healing, however, it is necessary to overhaul the fundamental worldview that determines the outlook and attitude that create the need to do violence to the organism in our manner of treatment—a manner that reflects the spirit of regarding disease as doing violence in equal measure such that we feel required to defeat and obliterate it.

One of the clearest examples of this predominant medical attitude is the one under discussion, the treatment of the acute "psychotic" episodes, holding the assumption that psychic events are ephemeral and vague as well as secondary spin-offs.

Biases like these filter out from the citadels of the medical clinics and laboratories to common people and families. In parents of psychotic offspring, one frequently finds the automatic assumption at work in the attitude toward the identified patient, that the entire trouble began with his or her faulty constitution. This occurs even in the face of volumes of clinical studies on the role of the family system in the etiology of psychosis.

To outgrow these biases far enough to recognize the self-healing elements in the psyche, even in the midst of the "psychotic" visionary states, it is not enough merely to enlarge one's information or to correct one's view by rethinking the question. For the consequences of such a change of viewpoint expand out to involve the entire fabric of one's understanding of human nature and the world, becoming too drastic an overturning of the foundations underlying one's view of the nature of reality to be comfortable. Even the challenge to put the psyche and its emotions on an equal footing with the body chemistry seems to be asking a bit too much.

I do not at all intend to imply that the persons undergoing a "psychosis" with world destruction and regeneration imagery emerge from their visions with a sophisticated new view of the nature of reality and time and space. They might. But what is revolutionary and pro-phetic in their cry for change is the constantly recurring picture of a world suffused with human-hearted caring, tolerance, and lovingness. That worldview is, after all, what is hoped for in the new consciousness recently stirring in our culture.

On the other hand, in choosing staff members for Diabasis, to accommodate "psychotic" visionary turmoils of this kind, we looked for people who appreciated such upheavals of worldview and who manifested the capacity for this kind of caring and loving. In such a sub-culture the tone of the client's visions would not fall on deaf ears, but would be met in a congenial setting with recognition of their import, thus to bring them into conscious living.

The undertaking of writing a book such as Dossey's on questions of healing, demonstrates very vividly the all-inclusive complexity of the current changes in worldview. Once one is willing to take a truly fresh and open look into this train of thought, soon a whole new experience of the nature of reality takes over; one is wandering in the terrain of a new physics, a new biology and biochemistry, a new neurology, and a new approach to medical treatment. These compose the province of the trans-personal consciousness with its many well-known scientific pioneers who are opening up this new understanding of the nature of reality.

Probing into the ultimate issues that invite this overhauling of worldview sets in motion a chain reaction involving basic psychic processes. This effort tends to activate the archetypal motifs we have been reviewing, dissolving one's old world-image and regenerating a new one that can meet the challenge to hold the elements of knowledge together in a new integration. In these present-day changes, the world "cannot be repaired, only recreated," to use Eliade's expression. If this happens to be felt as a comfortable rearrangement of one's thoughts, then the overhauling is probably not happening yet. It is far from a smooth reconsideration of one's intellectual outlook, but rather is a turbulent overturning of one's cherished, basic commonsense notion of the nature of things.

Einstein offered testimony to the anguish of these tribulations of mind:

> I must confess at the very beginning when the Special Theory of Relativity began to germinate in me, I was visited by all sorts of nervous conflicts. When young I used to go away for weeks in a state of confusion, as one who at that time had yet to overcome the state of stupefaction in his first encounter with such questions.[30]

An even more eloquent sketch of these trials is made by the physicist Pascua Jordan: in Dossey's paraphrase of it, he "described the agony of the physicists in the early years of the century, when the world of physics was convulsing. He stated that it was as if the earth itself had started trembling, and one did not know when it might completely disappear from under one's feet."[31]

A beautifully poetic account of an experience of the upheaval of world-image, with a somewhat romantic coloring, is rendered by

Herman Hesse in his late youth. In his *Incipit Vita Nuova*[32] he writes of a "point of transformation," a "place of terror and darkness":

> Shivering, I passed among the ruins of the world of my youth, over shattered thoughts . . . and everything I looked at dissolved into dust and ceased to live. . . . Everything that was still sacred and unravished and harmonious within me had lost its eyes and voice. . . . [A] spiritual derelict, I awoke to awareness of my misery . . . and like a hunted criminal who leaves his house at night, without taking leave and without closing the doors behind him. I departed from all the habits of my past. . . . My head reeled as I looked down into the abyss and found no end.

As the change came he "felt a swirling flood of gratitude, peace, and light and well-being" and then

> the position and recurrence of the heavenly bodies entered into a foreordained pact of friendship with my innermost life, and the eternal established a clear and soothing bond between its laws and something within me. I felt that in my life resurrected from the desert a golden foundation had been laid, a power and a law . . . everything old and new within me would forever after be ordered in noble crystalline forms and conclude beneficial alliances with all the things and wonders of the world. Incipit vita nuova. I became a new man.

Chapter 12

Visionary Experience in Myth and Ritual

Since the acute episode of visionary turmoil can have, along with its tormenting aspect, some ecstatic features, I will enlarge on the basic Dionysian principle that the exuberance of vital aliveness is born out of the realm of death. This is the miraculous revelation at the heart of the famous Dionysian rites, the Eleusinian mysteries.

Now this disturbing information is, in our American culture, very unwelcome news. Here ecstasy is desirable as long as it easy to attain. Yet, in truth, to have access to this state the price of admission is to take full account of the role of death. This is a difficult point, for we seem to find ourselves firmly biased against suffering and death as the ultimate enemy, dark and sinister, to whom we give no quarter and show no tolerance. You might say suffering and death are on an equal footing with madness in this respect.

We have seen that the growth process of the psyche, on the other hand, sees all this quite differently. According to the psyche's purposes, in order to break out of the security of solid consensus and convention, one must encounter the experience of the death process in psychic depth, and also at the same time the dissolution and destruction of the familiar, accustomed worldview. Though all this demand might seem at first glance overly drastic, it consists actually of the death of the familiar self-image and the destruction of the world-image to make room for the regeneration of each. These two images move together in the process, each an aspect of the other, and both assume the form of the mandala images.

I am going to illustrate the play of these images in three arenas: madness, creativity, and transformation. By madness I mean to imply "nonordinary states of consciousness" or "altered states" or "visionary states," but, of course, not to suggest the customary psychiatric condemnation of it as chaotic "disorder" with "bizarre ideation."

We should call to mind Plato's rendering of madness in his *Phaedrus*,[1] in which Socrates with delightful wit makes very clear the value of madness, of which he says there are two kinds: "one produced by human infirmity, the other by a divine release from the ordinary ways of men." The divine madness is of four kinds: prophetic, initiatory, poetic, and erotic—or, in our language for today's purposes: prophetic vision, ritual, creativity, and the love experience. Prophecy, he says, is a higher form than divination as is madness "superior to the sane mind, for the one is only of human, but the other of divine origin." The third kind of madness, creativity, "which is a possession by the Muses, enters into a delicate and virgin soul, and there inspiring frenzy, awakens lyric." With fervor and humor he adds, "But he who, not being inspired and having no touch of madness in his soul, comes to the door and thinks he will get into the temple by the help of art—he, I say, and his poetry are not admitted; the sane man is nowhere at all when he enters into rivalry with the madman."

Our star witness to this madness of all four kinds is Percy Bysshe Shelley and his "Prometheus Unbound,"[2] in which he shows himself master of rapture. "Why this?" one might ask, "Wasn't he just a dreamy romantic?" I had thought so until a full reading of him. In fact Shelley, as a vigorous and energetic revolutionary, advocated nonviolent confrontation expressly in the form picked up and put into effect by Gandhi; the poet wrote:

> Stand ye calm and resolute,
> Like a forest close and mute,
> With folded arms and looks which are
> Weapons of an unvanquished war.[3]
> ("The Masque of Anarchy")

He wrote of poets as the prophets of hidden futures. Poetry he, says, "is the faculty which contains within itself the seeds at once of its own and of social renovation. . . . Poetry could redeem the time . . . [and is] the source of whatever good . . . in an evil time." Poetry images "the children of airy hope, the prophets and parents of mysterious futurity."[4]

Significantly for our theme today, Shelley wrote "Prometheus Unbound" in a nonordinary, altered state of consciousness, wavering between suffering and ecstasy attributed to his tuberculosis but boosted with his use of laudanum. "My feelings," he wrote a friend at that time, "at intervals are of a deadly and torbid kind, or awakened to such a state of unnatural and keen excitement—that I find the very blades of grass and the boughs of trees present themselves to me with microscopic distinctness.[5]

The poem is a drama of transformation of the world by the overthrow of Jupiter, the prototype of kingship representing the tyrannical, repressive role of the Establishment as an evil power. Though instructed to rule wisely over gods and men, this high god violated his privilege, causing untold oppression and suffering for society. The titan Prometheus on the other hand becomes a savior transforming the world through his suffering on the icy rock to which he had been condemned by Jupiter; his punishment is turned into a redeeming empowerment.

Ecstatic visions abound in the drama. After Prometheus is released from his rock, he is seen undergoing his personal transformation by Panthea, the figure who represents Shelley's own visionary capacities. She describes a dream-vision of him thus:

> His pale wound-worn limbs
> Fell from Prometheus, and the azure night
> Grew radiant with the glory of that form
> Which lives unchanged within, and his voice fell
> Like music which makes giddy the dim brain,
> Faint with intoxication of keen joy.[6]

This corresponds, I suggest, to the death and renewal of the personified image of the Center. Panthea later perceives the transfiguration of the titan's consort, Asia, in corresponding manner:

> How thou art changed! I dare not look on thee;
> I feel but see thee not. I scarce endure
> The radiance of thy beauty . . .
>
> love like the atmosphere
> Of the sun's fire filling the living world,
> Burst from thee, and illumined earth and heaven
> And the deep ocean and the sunless caves.[7]

On the heels of these transformations comes that of the world itself with love predominating, without hierarchies of power, rigid institutions, or borders, or wars and contests for power.

Now the remarkable thing is that, though the drama itself ends there, in three acts, Shelley was not content to leave it at that. A fourth act celebrates the newly transformed world in a joyful cosmic dance of spirits. The dance then follows the pattern I have mentioned; the image of the self and that of the world move together. In this visionary rapture a play of circular forms appears mandala-like, with colors and lights all revolving in ecstatic vision with the accompanying music of the spheres:

After swift spirits are called from the depths of the sky and the ends of the earth, and the deep music of the rolling world makes itself heard, Panthea, the visionary, sees that from an opening in the wood

> Rushes, with loud and whirlwind harmony,
> A sphere, which is as many thousand spheres,
> Solid as crystal, yet through all its mass
> Flow, as through empty space, music and light:
> Ten thousand orbs involving and involved,
> Purple and azure, white, green and golden,
> Sphere within sphere; and every space between
> Peopled with unimaginable shapes . . .
>   and they whirl
> Over each other with a thousand motions . . .
> Kindling with mingled sounds, and many tones,
> Intelligible words and music wild.[8]

The Spirit of the Earth and the Spirit of the Moon now enter into dialogue in a love duet, and from the forehead of the former emanate forms

> Embleming heaven and earth united now.
> Vast beams like spokes of some invisible wheel
> Which whirl as the orb whirls, swifter than thought,
> Filling the abyss with sunlike lightnings,
> And perpendicular now, and now transverse,
> Pierce the dark soil, and as they pierce and pass,
> Make bare the secrets of the earth's deep heart.[9]

A truly Dionysian rapture now overtakes them:

> The joy, the triumph, the delight, the madness!
> The boundless, overflowing, bursting gladness,
> The vaporous exultation not to be confined![10]

Shelley at this point reveals his intention that this be understood as truly Dionysian frenzy in fact, for he has the moon sing,

> I, a most enamored maiden . . .
> Gazing, an insatiate bride,
> On thy form from every side.
> Like a Maenad,[11] round the cup
> Which Agave lifted up
> In the weird Cadmaean forest[12]

This ecstatic transformation of the world-image in Shelley's drama captures some of the essence of the creative process. I am reminded of things that Frank Barron said on the basis of a research project in Berkeley on the psychology of creative personalities (one I was fortunate enough to participate in and learn from). Frank Barron wrote in his own book on the topic some wise comments: the creative vision "requires an act of rejection breaking the previous world structure" . . . and it needs the work of the symbol "as the medium through which a superior vision of reality is sought, thus presenting a reality transcended."[13] In creative individuals, "We see frequently . . . an ability to transcend the ordinary boundaries of structures of consciousness . . . to break through the regularities of perception, to shatter what is stable or constant in consciousness, to go beyond the given world. . . . Such individuals are involved constantly in the creation of their private universes of meaning; they are cosmologists, all."[14]

When we reflect about the nature of creativity and its relation to madness, we should bear in mind the experimental work of Roland Fischer[15] on nonordinary, altered states of consciousness. For this he used certain psychoactive substances, in those years when one could still do such things, to investigate the array of various states of consciousness and provide a "cartography" of them. His model was an arc, the normative ego state at top center. To one side were states of increasing quiescence, as in Zen practice, reaching an empty consciousness until the ultimate point of enlightenment, the One. To the other side were states of increasing activation leading toward "high arousal states": first creativity, then anxiety, reaching then a "hyperphrenia" (a much more apt term for madness than "schizophrenia") characterized by high productivity of images and visions and ideation, until the ultimate point once more, of enlightenment, the One. We should note well here the continuum through creativity and madness finally to mystical states.

Of course, we must allow the modification that there is creativity to be found on either side of the arc, but of different kinds. Abraham Maslow[16] has described beautifully the creative process whose first phase is inspiration. This opening phase is a unitive state of absorption in the "matter at hand" so that the subject and object blend and lose differentiation; there results a state of bliss, of rapture. Herein is a moment of the Tao, in which one's receptiveness opens fully to the nature of the other and merges with it, thus most clearly perceiving the essence of the other. Now Maslow's description lies obviously in the direction of quiescence, in an absorbed concentration of consciousness. Here, however, I intend to follow the other side of the arc in the direction of the high arousal state, characterized by a turbulent outpouring of image content and emotion leading in the direction of wildness, of madness.

There is, then, in creativity a cosmological quality by which artists perceive the world newly, but there is also the function of prophetic vision, as Shelley so emphatically proposed. We have seen how much research among cultural anthropologists in recent decades has revealed that in various cultures in times of crucial, rapid culture change it is typical for great visionary prophets to behold overwhelming visions of cataclysm: the customary world is wiped out and a new one regenerated in new perfection.[17] Fresh myths and cults emerge out of these visions providing guidelines for the renewed culture. Poetry, prophecy, and visions of world regeneration tend to be linked together in a cluster, and to draw upon death and the realm of the dead for the reinvigoration of life.

To illustrate this clustering of motifs, I am going to draw upon a Norse myth having a quality far less ethereal than Shelley's and more darksome and stern. This is the *Voluspa*,[18] written by a medieval poet and based on still earlier material. The verses are put in the lips of the shamanic sybil or prophetess, telling of the god of poetry and inspiration of bards, called Odinn, and narrating his exploits and the last days of his world order.

My reason for turning attention at this point to Odinn is to bring into high relief the close relations between the creative process and the mythic motifs of world destruction and of the realms of death. The image of Dionysus carries these associations, but they are less clear in their outlines, while in the Norse myth they stand out dramatically.

Though in the Viking age Odinn became a god of warriors and kings, he derived from a more primordial historical level in which he showed affinities with both Dionysus and Shiva;[19] like them he caused states of intoxication and possession leading to ecstasy and poetic inspiration. We should envision Odinn as the living personification of an emotional state, *wut* (as his Teutonic name Wotan indicates),[20] which is a seizure of furor and raving, of wild excitement and frenzy. So to be possessed by this awesome divinity was to find oneself in ecstatic trance, by which one discovered the full dimensions of one's poetic genius.

As the Old Wanderer, Odinn was imaged as gray-bearded and one-eyed, with staff in hand, wearing a cloak and broad-brimmed hat. He was accompanied by two ravens and two wolves, creatures associated with death, for the realm of death was the source from which one learned wisdom. With this intent Teutonic poets would linger around burial mounds to receive inspiration from the deceased. Going quite a bit further than this, Odinn had the habit of hovering around graveyards and sitting under gallows to learn wisdom. This habit is to be understood as no mere lugubrious fancy on his part, but rather the earmark of the shaman in him.[21] The god's flying on his eight-legged horse, Sleipnir, to and from the land of death was typical of shamanic flight; on this airborne steed he led the wild hunt with his band of ghostly followers riding the winds and storms. The festival of this Allfather was the Yule, the winter solstice and darkest day of the year, when bands of his devotees dressed as wolves would rampage and maraud the countryside—hardly the "merry Yuletide" of our times!

Of great age and immense wisdom, Odinn was a psychopomp, a guide of souls, and even at the time of the creation itself it was he who gave breath and spirit to mankind. The god was said never to eat as even his wolves did, but to live only on the drinking of wine, and the mead from honey gave him wisdom and inspiration—here we can remind ourselves that though the Greek Dionysus was known for his patronage of wine, in his earlier Cretan years he was the master of the making of honey.[22] Out of this background, then, the source of poesy was known as "the cup of Ygg" and "mead of Ygg" (this being one of Odinn's names) and "the holy cup of the raven god."[23] For the ecstatic states from alcohol, mead, and poetry were considered holy since they put men in communion with the gods.

To return now to what the old prophetess, in the *Volupsa*, tells of the god, she narrates his venture of descent into the underworld to win the cup of poetic inspiration from the dwarf Mimir, by sacrificing to him his eye. The sybil also speaks of Odinn's ritual "sacrifice of himself to himself" to win the runes, which gave magic and oracular powers: this he carried out by hanging upon the great world tree, Yggdrasill, in the same manner that victims were hung on trees ritually as a sacrifice to him. Thus the name Yggdrasill has the connotation of the gallows of the god, Ygg, of Odinn. A famous verse[24] tells in Odinn's own words the story that he hung on the windy tree for nine nights, bearing the wound of a spear in the sacrifice of himself to himself. Looking down he clutched the runes with a cry and fell back. Thereupon he learned from a famous wise elder nine songs of power and won a draft of the precious mead that gave him the gift of poesy. In this way he found his extraordinary creativity growing by which words and actions came to him by their own spontaneity.

The theme of the world destruction is not merely an end point in the myth of Odinn, but is also linked to that of death throughout. The Allfather would arrange the death of his most heroic warriors in order to translate them over into the realm of the gods, to build up his armies in their magnificent palace of Valhalla. What might seem here like deceit in double-crossing his devotees, was in fact honoring them, for Odinn was choosing them for the very high honor of serving him in the final great war of the gods. The prophetess foretells the end of Odinn's order of the world of gods and men in this battle. There were to be three years of the monstrous winter, a sort of nuclear winter, freezing the world without pity and leading into the ultimate disaster of the Ragnarok, the final war between the gods and destruction of the world order. This apparent ending, though, was to be followed by a renewal of the world and its transformation into an age of benevolence.

In this darksome Norse myth I have obviously chosen an extreme example of the association of creative inspiration with the realm of death. While there are similarities between Odinn and Dionysus, they are also remarkably different. Both personify poetic inspiration, inducing frenzy and madness through possession and intoxication, especially by means of fermented honey, and both are deeply involved with the realm of death. The strongest contrast between these cults, though, is in the mood: there was a striking lack of joy and ecstasy in the Norse, where all was dark and heavy, and most particularly there was nothing of the feminine; the Greek cult was ecstatic and the god was tended primarily by women, whom he stole away from their accustomed life and seduced and loved.

Yet Dionysus, too, had darkness aplenty in his makeup, and to sketch this out I will draw upon and paraphrase the vivid account of him rendered by Walter Otto.[25] With the advent of Dionysus the primeval world comes to the fore and the depths open up with elemental forms of all that is creative and destructive, giving rise to both rapture and terror, even to the horror evoked by the uncanny. For Dionysus raves and makes mad, inciting even to savagery and lust for blood. Together with this lover's women, all are frenzied and swept up in wildness, in a wild spirit of the dreadful that mocks all institutions and creates instead bewitchment, ecstasy, and paralysis of all that is normative. For the routine world becomes shattered so that no illusions are left and only truth prevails, in that the usual dimensions of time and space lose their validity and laws lose their power. Dionysus strips mortals of all their conventions, of all that civilization holds dear, and hurls them into a life intoxicated by death. Bliss, enraptured and creative, shares in the madness. The god's name is also Bromios, designating the "din" raised by his following, the "loud shouter" of joy, with shrill instruments filling the air with the sound of flutes, drums, pipes, and cymbals.

Dionysus was also a "liberator," who revealed hidden things and the future, for at his shrines and festivals there lingered an atmosphere that was bewitched, filled with prophecy and miracles.

The essence of the god was Zoe, the mastery of life itself, a great cosmic enigma in its self-generating, self-creating properties; or as we would express it today, if we speak in the language of science, its self-organizing processes and in the terms of its own nature, the wonder of the vision that love gives rise to procreation and this in turn to madness.

What is said of procreation equally applies to creativity, and on this Otto speaks eloquently. The creative act never arises out of insufficiency, for on its threshold we are thrust out of all that is already known and thus secure and settled, out of every haven, and flung mercilessly into the primeval cosmic turmoil in which life is intoxicated with death. To beget something alive we dive into the primordial depths where the forces of Zoe dwell. When they rise to the surface, Otto says, there is a gleam of madness in the eye. The more alive life becomes, the nearer to death it draws, up to the supreme moment when the two join in an embrace.

In this train of thought I want to bring into the forefront some picture of the joyful, ecstatic aspect of the realm of death by briefly mentioning the near-death experience. Kenneth Ring[26] has done a painstaking labor of gathering a large sample of accounts of this state brought on by a variety of circumstances, producing actual clinical death for several minutes. Curiously, when the body is at its lowest possible ebb of energy, here the psyche finds itself at its peak in a high arousal state. Briefly to summarize some of the ecstatic occurrences in this condition, he stresses "(1) the incredible speed and sense of acceleration as one approaches (2) the light that (3) glows with overwhelming brilliance and yet (4) does not hurt the eyes." One feels in the presence of the light "(5) pure love, (6) total acceptance, (7) forgiveness . . . and (8) a sense of homecoming; that (9) communication with the light is instantaneous and nonverbal and that the light (10) imparts knowledge of a universal nature."[27] The love and the knowledge are to be recognized, we should note, as being of the same nature as the compassion and wisdom acclaimed in the great spiritual disciplines as the supreme goal of the mystical state.

One is reminded, in these accounts, of the Tantric Buddhist practice in the *Mahamudra* in which one enters and traverses the bardo states of the death experience. This meditation leads to the dissolution of the customary world and its recreation in the form of its perfection as a mandala. Needless to say, there takes place a dissolution of the customary self and its renewal into a state filled with love and wisdom.

After these many excursions into the various manifestations of the motifs of death, world destruction and renewal, and eruptions of the primordial mind in visionary states of possession, I wish now to draw them all together in citing the ultimate hyperphrenic state of madness, the acute "psychotic" episode (formerly called schizophrenia). Since a case presentation is out of the question here, I am going to create a composite picture of various visions and ecstatic experiences; I have gleaned these from a large number of persons in this state, ones that I have actually observed in the process of psychotherapy with "psychotic" persons.[28] I will call this the example of young Miss Allcase. As one hears these, one must keep reminding oneself that what makes the visions sound "crazy" is only her habit of identifying with each image as it makes its appearance on the stage of her inner world—otherwise the play of imagery is not so unnatural.

Young Miss Allcase is twenty-eight or thirty. For a few days she has withdrawn into her inner thoughts and ruminations, which have led her to eat and sleep too little. She has been convinced she is dying and gradually the outer world is looking increasingly unreal, and the sense of reality has been shifting instead to the mythic, inner primordial world. She has spent the night in the position of the crucifixion with pains pulling at her chest toward either side, and the feeling of death is sweeping over her.

In the morning she believes herself to be in the Garden of Eden and to be Eve herself, and somehow also her daughter. This place is the center of the world and time has swung back to the beginnings of time. She has been sensing odors of death, from the Devil, and all the people around her are dead like herself, dwelling in the afterlife. In visions she beholds the creation going on in space, its very first moments, with little rings of light coalescing into planets. But she feels overwhelming fears about these events because there are evil forces in the cosmos that wish to destroy the world. These powers take the form of political ideologies competing for control, in two, three, and then four factions. All the issues of life seem to be falling into opposites, and worse, the usual order of things goes topsy-turvy, and she is seized with a mortal fear of being turned into a man. Her sense of who she is swells to immense proportions, and with an uprush of emotion she knows herself to be the goddess and creatrix of moon and stars; she and the world are one, for she is old Earth Mother herself. In a vision she and a lover are royal twins, King and Queen of the Universe, who with another couple stand each on a globe forming four planets in a cosmic circle. At night she participates in sexual embrace with God and by this union conceives a new divine child, a redeemer who will save the world. She experiences many forms of birth out of death, and this becomes associated with the resurrection, allowing her to recognize what death is about. She feels a strong creative urge to write, redoing the Bible and pronouncing a new message of love. In a dramatic vision she watches the world being transformed: the San Francisco Bay drops down to become a new Hell and a new regime arrives from outer space to establish the New Heaven and New Earth—at its center the city becomes a New Jerusalem, a City of Peace with a golden palace at its midpoint. She sees many images of the world quadrated in four continents, factions, creeds, and races, or surrounded by four planets; four powers clash at the center and all goes dark, but the sun comes out again over them and they make peace and learn to live in harmony.

All these colorful visions are known to psychiatry as "bizarre ideation," but in that case the same would have to be said of the myths and rituals of Dionysus and Odinn, and of Shelley's "Prometheus Unbound." In consequence my main concern in the 1990s is the question: What do we do with our visionaries? When the divine madness takes them over the point of distress and disorientation, we pull them out of it with isolation and medication to squelch by every means this process at its start. It is clear that society is hostile to whatever deviates from the baseline of normative experience—too much excursion up or down evokes a swift corrective and forcible return to "normal." However, if we live always at this baseline, always doing only what we are supposed to do and remaining safe, then no vision, no ecstasy, and no Dionysus! Dionysus becomes locked out, but we then find ourselves left inside the prison of safe security and consensus, and Dionysus remains free to possess whom he will.

Part III

Summary in Respect to Spiritual Emergency

I have repeatedly been puzzled by the extreme turbulence that accompanies profound change in the psyche. When a true spiritual awakening or transformation is under way, one usually encounters the emotional experiences and accompanying images of death and of the annihilation of the world itself. The psyche is not gentle in its expressions. One would like to expect that these movements of the spirit should come about by educational means of a more genteel nature, with instruction, workshops, exercises, and other modes of gradual change in orderly sequence. Depth work in psychotherapy holds the hope that it might bring about this change in a more kindly fashion; but even there, as Jung has observed,[1] there are passages in the work in which there occur very uncomfortable states of de-adaptation along the way and episodes of altered states of consciousness that can even be called transitory "psychosis" that are mild and short.

The question is, then: Why the need for all this upheaval? There are good reasons that rest upon a second query: What is spirit and what is its nature?

People often use the word *spiritual* loosely to signify something uplifting, like high-level thought; at the extreme it is spoken of as lofty, seraphic, and rarefied, high above nature as though in some other realm, hence supernatural. One knows better how it looks and feels when one experiences it at work! In descriptions of cultures, the word is often used to designate those aspects that are not merely material, economic, or political.

When we look at the actual phenomenology of spirit, we get a different impression. The ancient words for this give us a lead, for they imply breath or air, particularly air in motion, and thus wind; in Hebrew *ruach*, in Greek *pneuma*, in Latin *animus*, in the far East *prana* or *ch'i*, and so on. The word *spirit* itself conveys the meaning of breath, derived from the Latin *spiritus*. All these terms clearly denote a dynamism that is invisible as air but capable of being powerful as wind. It "bloweth where it listeth" the Gospel says,[2] suggesting that it has a will of its own. In short, spirit is a strongly moving dynamism free of material structure.

These pointers lead us to think of this dynamism as a pure energy, but on closer look we find it a bit more than that—it is typically experienced as having a voice, as when persons are moved by the spirit. It seems then to have the property of intention and to be freighted with information. In this aspect we could think of it as "informed energy" or energy with the quality of mind.

Following this line of consideration, spirit cannot be separated from its plural form, "spirits." In old traditional societies these are invisible dynamisms that live as denizens of the natural world, especially of biological life, but also mountains, streams, and springs, in a belief system called "animistic." To clairvoyants these spirits appear not only to have a voice but also to take on a personified visibility. These beings require a great deal of attention from the human community in the form of offerings and sacrifices. When one lives in such a society, as I have in China, one is made constantly aware of this other dimension of existence, one that here in the West we have long since relegated to oblivion.

Less unusual in sophisticated cultures are experiences with spirits considered to belong to the realm of the afterlife, the deceased. In this case death is viewed as a liberation of the spirit from its housing in its former this-worldly structure, the body, by a transformation process of transfiguration. In China, for example, "Heaven" has been revered as a presence, presiding over the affairs of the world, consisting of a conglomerate of ancestral spirits (royal ones) and being possessed of intention and will. In ancient traditions all over the world, spirits are highly valued ancestral beings that make themselves heard, give advice and counsel, and even make demands. When visiting black communities in Africa I was amazed at their constant attention to these spirits as a matter-of-fact part of their day-to-day life. Ever since I have been questioning what to make of them psychologically.

From this extremely cursory glance at the range of manifestations of spirit and spirits, we may glean that spirit can be either free of bodily structure or can tend to be liberated from it. This I find helpful toward understanding how spirit operates in psychological experience. For here again we find spirit tending constantly to seek release from its entrapment in habitual, routine, or conventional mental structures. Spiritual work is one of liberating this dynamic energy, which must break free of its suffocation in old forms: old emotional patterns, such as the complexes engendered in the family system; assumptions about the nature of the world and human life; values that need revision from time to time as conditions change; and cultural forms derived from family, subculture, or dominant cultural conditionings that must change with the times. Again there are ancient traditions expressing this work of liberating spirit, such as the emotionally painful labors of the nature philosophers of medieval times dedicated to freeing *nous* from *physis*, spirit from imprisonment in matter—in the natural world and in the body.

In our times, if during a person's developmental process this work of releasing spirit becomes imperative, but is not undertaken voluntarily with knowledge of the goal and with considerable effort, then the psyche is apt to take over and overwhelm the conscious personality with its own powerful processes. I have observed these in a large number of cases of acute "psychosis," which I have formulated and called the renewal process.[3]

For our present purposes I am focusing on two components of this sequence of motifs that highlight its disintegrative and reintegrative aspects: the emotional experiences and images of death and world destruction.

Whenever a profound experience of change is about to take place, its harbinger is the motif of death. The question why is not particularly mysterious, since it is the limited view and appraisal of oneself that primarily must be outgrown. This issue is compacted in the self-image, and to accomplish its transformation it must dissolve in the manner of death, to be renewed. In severe visionary states, one may feel that one has crossed over into the realm of death and is living among the spirits of the deceased. In this one is being forced to let go of old expectations of oneself and to let oneself be tossed about by the winds of change.

Far less familiar is the companion piece to this death motif: the image of world destruction. Like the self-image, the world-image is a compacted form of the very complex pattern of how one sees the world and how one lives in it. We learn most about this from cultural anthropologists, who find that, in times of acute and rapid culture change, visionaries undergo the somewhat shattering experience of seeing the world dissolve into a chaos and time whirl back to its beginnings.[4] This dissolution of the world-image clearly represents the death of the old culture to pave the way for its renovation. The same applies in the case of an individual's life: when a transformation of one's inner culture is under way dissolution of the world-image is the harbinger of change. During this process expressions of cultural reforms are explicit.

These and other archetypal affect-images[5] have the function of implementing the processes of the spirit: of liberating and transforming its energies, which will then slip out of the old structures lingering on from the recent past and into new ones geared to the near future. All this happens in the interests of development, that is, of cultivating a more capacious consciousness, open to dimensions of experience that it had been closed to before. Not only are these two motifs, self-image and world-image, companion pieces in the process, but they also share the same image for their representation: the mandala.[6] The entire process of renewal evidently is the work of this powerful affect-image representing the psyche's governing Center.

Needless to say, the energy that has been bound up in the structures of the old self-image and world-image—in the issues of what one is and what sort of world one lives in—has to be immense. In dreams or visions, nuclear explosion is a frequent expression of its release.[7] The enormous charge of psychic energy is on the loose during the renewal process and raises havoc for a period. Though one's own proper nature is struggling to break through, one may feel that who one is and what one's values are, seem to be up for grabs for a while. Indeed, the values and emotional issues of life all seem to fall into division as clashing opposites.

Yet the energy does not remain long in suspense, but quickly seeks its reincarnation into new structures, expressed in the form of images and experiences of rebirth and world regeneration. A new sense of oneself appears along with fresh interests and motivations in the world. The new birth activates one's memory of the actual events of one's first birth, thus linking these phenomena with those studied by Stanislav Grof.[8] Following upon this also occurs an inner reenactment of emotional experiences of early years.

The cataclysm of this kind of crisis in spiritual processes always reminds me of the biblical warning, "It is a fearful thing to fall into the hands of the living God,"[9] because in the intermediate time between the initial visions of death and world destruction and their resolution in renewal, one is apt to be caught in the grip of fear. There is dismay over finding oneself in isolation inasmuch as communication of one's experiences is usually not received empathetically. Just at the time one is seized with an inordinate need for loving reception, one finds oneself instead either alone with it or surrounded by professionals who want to suppress what is happening and make one conform to the ways of the former self and former world.

The fear of this and the accompanying rage naturally produce biochemical effects in the brain and the rest of the body, leading those who prefer the medical model to find in these changes the primary cause of the "disorder." This mechanistically biased view does not hold up, however, since it is now well known that if the person undergoing this turmoil is given a loving, understanding, and encouraging reception it may resolve in a short time without the need for its interruption by suppressive medication. The most fragmented "thought disorder" can become quite coherent and orderly within a few days if there is someone at hand to respond to it in a spirit of real, honest, and warm relatedness. Such a relationship affords a far better container than a tranquilizer in most instances. A haven where there is attentiveness to inner experience can also be of great advantage, where one can overhaul one's life away from its usual context. Loren Mosher has demonstrated by scrupulously thorough research the effectiveness of these methods in Soteria, a low-cost residential facility in the 1970s that emphasized relationship instead of medication.[10]

I have been dwelling on the more extreme forms of visionary states because the deep psychic process is so much out in the open that one can learn much to help understand its nature. The more usual form of spiritual emergence, while showing the same psychic contents and processes, may be far less disruptive. There is a broad range of severity from the horrendous to the mild, depending perhaps on how vigorous the resources of a person's consciousness are and how rich in its repertory one's unconscious psyche might be. The handling of it is the same in one respect though: the process of renewal needs a partner.

What turns out to be the ultimate goal of spiritual emergence and the renewal process? I think the most concise way of putting it is that it is the same as that of the mystic way or of meditation, which is phrased in Buddhist practice as wisdom and compassion (love). These are what emerge in the process and what are required of the partner in the work.

For most persons the very moment of slipping over the edge into the onslaught of confusion and welter of visionary images is marked by the experience of dying and entering the afterlife. Leading up to this crucial point there usually has been a gradual shift of attention from involvement with the conventional reality to concerns with that other reality, the inner life. What this signifies psychologically is that at this point of the break, there occurs a dramatic drop of energy out of the conscious field simultaneously with an intense activation of the archetypal level of the deep psyche with its profusion of mythic imagery. This surcharge of energy produces what Roland Fischer calls the "high arousal state."[11] Such psychological terms are adequate for a dispassionately objective account of these events, but for the subjective side one must think in the language of overwhelming cataracts of mythic ideation and symbolic forms. In this state every occurrence seems to conjure up a multiplicity of meanings.

The particular component in the psyche that shows itself to be the focus of this activation and energy is the archetype of the Center, that which Jung has described as the Self, representing itself in quadrated

circles, quadripartite circles and mandalas.[12] The course of the process
and the accompanying imagery point to this Center as that which is
being renewed, and all the parts and phases of the renewal represent
themselves as taking place within this Center as their vessel of
transformation.

I have described elsewhere the components and phases of the
renewal process and their myth and ritual in antiquity.[13] The process has
a venerable history of five thousand years. In both individuals of today
and cultures of antiquity it has taken the form of ritual drama:

Briefly spoken, a world center is established. In this locus, there
follows upon the experience of death and the afterlife a regression of
time back to the beginnings: in the case of a person's past, back to the
mother, whether as her infant, or to the breast, or to one's birth or even
one's intrauterine state; or in the larger dimension of the world's past,
back to the creation or even back to the state of chaos before it. The self-
image and the world-image thus reflect each other and run in parallel
through this sequence. However, all does not move with easy assurance
through this reenactment of the beginnings: the opposites become
vividly constellated, especially those that strive to destroy all existence,
entering a cosmic conflict and combat against those benign forces that
would preserve it and effect a world regeneration. Along with these,
opposites of every kind tussle for ascendancy. Among these one pair that
is quite distressing to the individual is the rousing of the contrasexual
component, with feelings of being changed into the other sex (not to be
construed necessarily as homosexual panic).

So far, these are mostly heavy, frightening, even nightmarish
elements in the progress of renewal; further ones are apt to have a more
high mood to them. There is the inflated image of oneself in an
apotheosis as hero or heroine, saint, savior, messiah, or king. In this
capacity one has at some point the experience of being brought into a
hieros gamos, a sacred or heavenly marriage with some mythic or divine
figure, with all the accompanying exhilaration and upsurge of erotic
emotion. Also in the messianic role one believes oneself specially elected
to bring about reforms of religion or society on a world scale, thus
bringing into effect a significant aspect of the world regeneration. By the
same token, the self-image is renewed in the manner of a rebirth, or
sometimes new birth, brought about by the fruitful event of the sacred
marriage,

Through all this interplay of opposites one may, then, discern their
clashing, their reversing one into the other, and their union. In the
drawings and paintings that often emerge in profusion to express these
inner events, each of these elements in the process tends to be staged

within the mandala form representing the archetypal Center, the Self, well known as the container of opposites.[14]

"But wait a minute," one might object. "In spiritual practices isn't the Self something that's transcendent and eternal? How can it be going through death and disintegration? Isn't it the ego that's supposed to go through a sacrificial death?" In answer we look to myth and ritual to give us the authoritative word.

An example is found in the Christian tradition in which Christ was the incarnation of the eternal godhead and the representation of the Self; his death and transfiguration became the way the process of renewal was symbolized in that faith. Baptism, for example was originally an initiation "into the death of Christ"[15] and thus into his spiritual kingdom of which he was king. During the preceding three millennia there was a gradual development of the ceremonial of the sacral kingship of the ancient Near East;[16] these royal functionaries, as delegates of the deity and personifications of the Center, submitted themselves to an annual death-and-renewal in the great communal festivals of the New Year. It is in these that we find the close parallels to the renewal process occurring in individuals today. One might think of the dying gods—Baal in the Near East, Adonis in the Mediterranean cultures, or Freyr in the Nordic—as vegetation and fertility spirits, but each of these names is translated "Lord" in the royal connotation, implying similarly the role of the Center.

On this account the recent prevalent emphasis on ego-cide or ego death is apt to miss the essential point, for these terms imply a consciously willed event. The truly transformative death comes usually unbidden if not unwelcome, of itself, happening to us and in spite of us. It is an autonomous and archetypal process among ritual images, as a movement of the spirit in the realm of myth and ritual.

It seems to be in the nature of the archetypal Center to undergo cyclic rounds of birth, death, and resurrection. This process used to be quite conscious to the people of ancient or archaic cultures. Yet somehow it has become alien and more unconscious to us moderns, who are prone to be enamored of linear progress (if there is any such thing) or of an abiding divine presence that somehow manages to avoid the cyclic world of nature in which this spirit lives and works.

Any contradiction in all of this I think can be resolved if we refine our understanding of the difference between the archetypal Center itself on one hand and the image that represents it on the other. The image in this sense does not signify merely its picturing, but rather the form and quality that it takes in our actual experience. If I may be allowed to share my own experience as an example of the point, when my analytic exploration of depth was going on in my analysis, this center was frequently depicted in dreams in the form of nonordinary mandala-shaped churches, my spiritual upbringing having come in the context of the Anglican Church. Shortly later dreams announced a shake-up in this cultural set: a scene revealed the fate of Westminster Abbey, the heart of the Anglican Church, in its becoming a delicate, exquisite, but empty Gothic shell of stone, while a guide pointed to mysteriously shaped and colored mountains of China as the area where the numinous, living spirit now resides (such mountains mark the Center and four cardinal points of the Chinese world). My worldview is now more Taoist than Christian.

The archetypal Center abides but the image representing it is what needs renewal cyclically, with all that this implies about the outlook, lifestyle, and value system by which one lives. The only way we are capable of apprehending the Center, then, is through its embodiment in images (or visions of light), and these are periodically transformed in the psyche's development: no form that it takes is static. The individuating psyche abhors stasis as nature abhors a vacuum; the spirit shuns imprisonment in nongrowing forms or structures. The Taoists understand very well that opposites, good and bad, beautiful and ugly, are not real entities in themselves but, like the Yin and Yang, are in perpetual flux revolving around the Center after one another in their alternations of ascendance and yielding, while the Tao at the Center abides without name or definition.

From time to time, a form of the Self is designated by a certain symbolic or mythic image that captures the dynamic essence of that phase of a person's life, until it has done its work and its hour has come to be dissolved. The person does sense something dying, but the ego changes only secondarily to the demise of the image of the Self, the Center. What happens in the ego reflects the dynamisms in the archetypal psyche. Of the two levels of the self-image, the archetypal one in depth effects transformations, while the personal one in the conscious personality reflects these changes. Then the reorganization of the Self of which we are speaking occurs on both these levels.

Just as there are some regularities, as I have described, in the elements in this renewal process, there is also a shift in direction and outcome similarly to be expected. Customarily it gets under way with a predominance of images and feelings of prestige and power, much of which seems compensatory to a debased self-image, a low opinion of oneself; these images also can be said to reflect the idiom of the family subculture in which the person was raised, to his or her detriment. But during the weeks of the process, it appears usually to move in the direction of stirring up the motivations and capacities that lead to lovingness and compassion. I feel these to be the prime fruit of the work of the spirit, as its chief and crowning goal. This may be experienced both as warmth and intimacy moving into one's relationships, and also as a direct sense of the oneness of all beings—not just as a belief or view of how things are, but as the actual experiential realization of it.

This aspect of the process has evolutionary implications. Among the myth and ritual parallels one can trace in history the rise of this human-hearted capacity into cultural awareness and expression, displacing a previous predilection for dominance and violence—in the mid-first millennium B.C.E. this occurred in those several parts of the world in which cultures survived a sufficient number of centuries for them to attain their fulfilled maturity.[17] This human-heartedness is in Jungian terms the Eros mode of relating to the world, over against the Logos that becomes the Power mode when it seeks to dominate and control. It operates according to the receptive, a principle that motivates us to open ourselves fully to the nature and needs of the world around us.

Since it is in the nature of spirit to renew its expression in archetypal form, and in doing so to cause considerable disruption of the customary conscious adaptation by robbing its energy, favorable conditions are required in which to handle this transition during its progress of several weeks.

The psyche has its own natural way of seeking privacy in a space set apart, in separation, by withdrawal. This is disapproved of psychiatrically, yet ritual procedures have always established sacred enclosures for renewal processes to allow a clear differentiation of sacred and secular; what transpires in such sanctuary goes by different rules. So perhaps the term *retreat*, with all that it implies of this sort of apartness, is more fitting than *withdrawal*. One good reason for such safe asylum is that the usual input from the mundane is positively painful to persons in this state of high arousal if too strong in sensory or emotional stimuli. Even more urgently the customary input can be confusing since one is dwelling at such a time in a mythic world totally out of keeping with the mundane. This is an archaic way of experience, quite overt and conscious in the ancient cultures of five thousand years ago but deeply unconscious in today's.

The confusing discrepancy between the ordinary and the nonordinary worlds causes as much distress to people in the surroundings of a person in this state as it does to the person. A mutually frightening gulf opens up between them and requires comfortable bridging. On this account, not only are sanctuary and a homelike atmosphere desirable, but in such a residence the most important element is the reception the staff offer the client, that is, the staff's "take" on the state of mind in which the client is caught.

First and foremost in the policy of Diabasis was the requirement that all members agree on a nonsickness view of this dramatic turmoil. This goes nowadays by the name of "nonlabeling." It means that the staff must be made up of persons who honestly know what is a meaningful inner process and what is pathology; it is not enough to take it on hearsay, or to have a correct and liberal intellectual view, but requires something in their actual life that allows them to know experientially. Otherwise when it comes to the crunch in a moment of crisis the truth of this knowing comes out in bold relief. This process does need a name, though, in order to be able to talk about it, so the point is to avoid names with damaging implications and to use ones that actually connote this state.

Since the process involves a renewing of the Self and the self-image, the next matter of importance is the staff's ability to respond to the newly emerging person with genuine caring, with a loving appreciation of the qualities coming to light. A sensitive discrimination between what is a person's essence and what is the dross, derived from the accidents of upbringing, does much to foster the next steps in his or her development.

By the same token, inasmuch as the process tends to shift from motivations of power and prestige to ones of love and relatedness, this newly emerging capacity must be met with responses in kind—there can then be a real joining with the person's upcoming tenor of feeling. A facility based on the principles of law-and-order, so prevalent in the hierarchically organized hospital wards, is self-defeating, or may I say, Self-defeating! It is too closely a reenactment of the schizogenic family setting, the initial faulty starting point.

For these requirements, then, the selection of staff personnel departs from the usual habits of assessment. This way one chooses according to personal qualities, not professional qualifications, that is, the categorical prerequisites of education and training. The attributes that make good members are a sensitive receptiveness and a respect for another person's quite different mental state, experience, and, especially, private space; there is a subtle quality of nonintrusive allowingness to be sought. As already mentioned, it is advisable to pick people who have "been there" in some form or another—if only through therapy. Obviously a non-cerebral vitality and warmth of responsiveness are part of the picture of a member who would be capable of empathy and honest, clean emotional interactions.

Such a staff forms a community that is real, that is, open and close with one another and devoted. They become capable of declaring their honest feeling and experience of whatever kind, and of straightforward expression of these toward each other and the clients. It is into this atmosphere that the client enters from the start, and one has only to witness the effect this has upon him or her to realize how vital it is to have things set up this way; a disturbed person can come down from utmost confusion into clarity within a few days. The intent is not merely to be humane and "nice" to clients—it is all geared to the earnest business of discovering selfhood.

At Diabasis a significant part of this policy was the declaration at the start that there were no "experts"—everyone was open to learning and discovering. We had our several gifts and accumulations of experience of various kinds to provide. In the same spirit, we had no bosses, no government from the top. The whole community of staff was the policymaker. Individuals had skills and applied them in the spirit of effective division of labor; this included administrators and psychiatrists. The entire project was viewed as the creation by the staff out of their own vision and effort, and as belonging to them. Quickly I must qualify this in mentioning that the matters of legal liability, and hence of board accountability, came in question at the time when our funds were being denied and we were being closed in 1979, and therefore they were not solved. The advantages of this policy, however, were clearly evident: the sense of responsibility for the entire house rested in each member, not in some chief, so that at crucial moments of decision and choice of action in the work itself, each felt entitled to act with freedom of judgment. Each represented Diabasis and its way; the whole was represented in the parts, and thus our little microcosm reflected the nature of the macrocosm!

The concept of a therapeutic mode like this, no matter how disturbed the person, is that in the high arousal state when the archetypal unconscious is energized and activated, the psyche does its own work in its own fashion. What is needed for this is not "treatment" but rather a coming into close and deep relationship with an other, with an individual staff member who empathizes and encourages but does not interfere. This partnership provides a container that is far more effective than medication. It also offers the opportunity for the individual to concentrate on the inner work, keeping it sustained and moving forward in the process. Without such a relationship there is a tendency for the communication to be highly fragmented and for the process to get stuck, going round and round the same contents without progress. As I see it, the need for a partner in the work springs from the fact the archetypal Self or Center tends in general to become activated in intense relationship and to need that emotional framework in order to progress along the path of its renewal process.

So in these circumstances, with all the expression in art forms that pours out so readily, the other is expected to be responsive to it; or in the rage room the impulse to lash out and destroy is given safe space and is conveyed to the other in relationship. The past with all its hurts and fears and angers becomes intensely reenacted in the sessions between the two persons, from birth to the present often, and profoundly healing things take place.

In mentioning, above, the role of visionary experiences in culture change, I was pointing up the analogy it provides for an understanding of the renewal process in individuals. I now want to reverse this emphasis and show how such personal experiences throw light upon the evolution of cultures.

When I first began the study of the ideation in cases of "psychosis," I was puzzled by the marked prevalence of political ideology. There seemed to be fully as much involvement in these societal concerns as in early family relations. Their world-image went through sequences that differentiated four sections of the globe representing races, colors, creeds, and political persuasions, first clashing in conflict and then being resolved into harmonious integration. The possibility of world destruction was a theme running through this development.

Some time elapsed before I realized that these phenomena were in line with the findings of cultural anthropologists in regard to the issues of acculturation. Culture change occurs in two main ways: by slow increments without major transformations of *ethos* and *eidos*, of values and meanings; or by acute, rapidly moving upheavals that overhaul the basic outlook and lifestyle. The myth-making in this rapid culture change is customarily the work of visionaries and prophets who personally undergo turmoils similar to those of persons in "psychotic" visionary states, seeing themselves dead and beholding the world being shattered by fire, storm, flood, or earthquake. They initiate spiritual movements with new myths portraying major advances in consciousness and way of life. The psychic events leave little room for doubt that the visions of the end of the world signify the demise of the culture that is being outgrown, and the world regeneration that follows, its renovation in a new pattern. These cataclysmic spiritual turning-points are evolutionary leaps produced by the psyche in its own particular fashion through the renewal process.

The spirit, then, moves toward its objectives by turmoils and upheavals, and evolution advances by leaps. By now I regard the acute "psychotic" visionary state as the psyche's effort to renew an individual's cultural set. It appears that this may be intended primarily for one's own spiritual growth and development of personality, unless there happens to be an exceptional giftedness or calling. In this case, when one is endowed with the ability for fine articulation and with the attendant charisma, then one may have much to offer to one's culture for its spiritual growth and development.

If this way of viewing psychic turmoils is on target, then there is grave danger in psychiatry's zeal to suppress them, and instead there is an urgent need to safeguard visionary experience for the benefit of the culture.

This is a time when the Eros mode and the receptive principle in relating to the world are drastically needed for our spiritual evolution. This age is similar to the first millennium B.C.E. in this respect, one in which great visionaries recognized the role of compassion in the ordering of society and the role of wisdom in new world visions that took into account the whole of existence, the One. We see now again the picture of the collective psyche thrusting up to move forward and implement the work of the spirit through various cultural avenues.[18] At such a crucial turning point the renewal process has much work to do and requires visionary experience for its accomplishment.

Appendices

Appendix A
Addendum Queries on Chapter 8

Dr. Burton: Since your chapter deals with the most difficult behavior change of all, the psychotherapy of schizophrenia, would you first indicate what you believe a psychosis to be and, secondly, what schizophrenia is in particular?

Dr. Perry: Acute psychosis is a state in which, as Jung has suggested, the dream takes the place of reality. That is, the sense of reality shifts from the outer to the inner world or stage of experience. This is brought about by the circumstance that the ego-consciousness has become overwhelmed by the archetypal affect- images of the unconscious; in the case of depression, by the affects, in the case of schizophrenia, by the images. I cannot see this condition as arising out of a defense against reality, or any other defensive maneuver. It seems rather that the whole syndrome represents instead a shift of the energy so activating the unconscious psyche that it deprives the ego-consciousness of its usual charge. To me it appears that the more acute the psychotic state, the more are the defenses overridden altogether.

I see the acute "schizophrenic" episode, after working with it for over twenty years, as a high arousal state in which the lower centers and functions are activated at the cost of the higher. It is more realistically viewed as an altered state of consciousness than as a play of psychopathology. A comparison of its phenomenology with parallels in the altered states that are culturally accepted in various societies leads me to call it a "visionary state."

This hyperactivation of the unconscious functions also appears in the phenomenology as emerging from the affect-image that represents itself as the Center, the archetypal image described by Jung as the Self, which I prefer to call the "central archetype." The highly dynamic process that this center undergoes robs the higher structures and functions of their customary energy, leaving both the ego-consciousness and the autonomous complexes in a state of fragmentation, and giving rise to the characteristic earmarks of the syndrome, the "thought disorder" and the apparent "dulling of the affect."

The intent of the activation of the archetypal Center is observable if one follows the mental content with care. It shows itself to be the psyche's effort to refashion and renew its cultural orientation, value system, and world-image, that is, its entire structure of values, meanings and design of life. Hence the acute process is so comparable with prophetic and messianic visionary states in rapid culture change as to be indistinguishable.

II

Dr. Burton: Empathy and clarification of feeling are important aspects of the mandatory openness in your therapy with psychotic patents. But I have seen situations where such therapeutic "flowing" led to increased anxiety and autism in the patient. Is there perhaps a still additional factor in the personality of the therapist or in his or her situation which catalyses empathy and clarification and signals them as curative? The empathy and clarification of encounter groups, for example, have never seemed to me sufficient as curative means.

Dr. Perry: In my experience, the increase in anxiety or autism with this sort of therapy may occur in two kinds of situations. Many persons with a paranoid style of makeup resist the inner vision as a subjective experience and desperately strive to keep it externalized, feeling severely threatened if it is brought too close to inner experience. Also in the chronic condition, after the acute visionary state had been undergone and had failed to do its work, a person may be left with only a fear of its recurrence as a sort of nightmare. In both these situations, I feel we as therapists should be willing to admit the possibility that they are the results of our own failure to know how to deal with the acute episodes in various kinds of personality.

The additional factors in the personality of the therapist who can work in this fashion are, as I have found them, openness and sensitivity to subjective events, and a capacity for the "informed listening" that arises from some sort of personal experience with the inner life of psychic depth. These allow an open receptivity without being overwhelmed by anxiety, and also allow an honesty and freedom of emotional and conceptual response, including even an affectionate intimacy. I feel group relations cannot take in this dimension of fullness in the client's experience because the emphasis must be upon group process and not the subtle inner process going on in psychic depth; it seems very hard to reveal this inner part except to one person at a time, where confidence is unstinting.

III

Dr. Burton: People who do psychotherapy with schizophrenic patients, myself included, have been accused of romanticizing a truly malevolent psychopathology and its cure. It is of course not even certain that schizophrenia may not turn out to be an organic disease or a secreting toxin, as Jung finally thought. Do you sometimes feel that the encounter with a schizophrenic patient, as described in your chapter, is a poetic rather than a medical thing and that a two-way idealization is somewhat involved?

Dr. Perry: When the question is raised that this may be fundamentally a condition of biochemical origin, as much of today's psychiatric literature would have us believe, we need to remind ourselves that any emotional occurrence has its biochemical as well as its psychic aspect. It would not occur to me as a psychotherapist to say that I fear a monster in a nightmare because my autonomic nervous system's chemistry induces in me the disturbance (James and Lange notwithstanding). In other words, if one were to have a shattering experience of God, I do not believe one could detect a millisecond's lag between the mental and the physical state, to indicate primacy in time and causation. That is why I prefer to call these phenomena "affect-images." The whole organism operates as a unity—psyche and soma—and any claim to give priority to one over the other seems to me motivated by the bias of a certain culture that somehow views somatic events as "real" and their psychic equivalent as "mystical," meaning misty. This view of mine is in harmony with Jung's that you mention, since he suggested that a toxin might be produced by the hyper-activity of a disturbing autonomous complex; this never held him back from handling schizophrenia by a conscientious psychotherapy, which would in turn diminish the toxin.

In my opinion the malevolent course of schizophrenia, which occurs often enough, is probably in most instances an outcome of our way of handling it (Jung made this observation also as far back as 1914). "Schizophrenia" is strangely chameleonlike, appearing very differently in different surroundings. Better said, it is like a magic mirror that reflects back to us exactly what we expect to see; in this regard it behaves just the way the archetypal unconscious does, which, if we approach it with fear becomes fearsome, with hostility, hostile, or with awe, awesome. We can always find our expectation justified somehow. Thus if one in an eighteenth-century manner anticipates bestiality, the psychotic feels and acts bestial; if one expects a violent and insane behavior, one has a wardful of patients acting out violently and needing heavy control; if one's view is that this is a degenerative disease, as in the first decades of this century, then one finds many of one's patients showing a downhill course. In the same way, if one sees in this syndrome nature's own way of effecting change, then this is what takes place in the larger number of cases. At Diabasis we gave a realistically favorable but not idealized picture of what our clients were going through, and hence we had a community of clients who needed no medication to feel sane again within two to five days, and who enjoyed their stay; the atmosphere was spirited, even jovial often; conversations were lively; people were fond of each other; and most were at work on their inner process.

The tenor of the work does have much of the poetic about it, inasmuch as one is dealing most of the time with metaphorical expressions of the deep and underlying issues of our lives and our culture. These are images that, to use Sullivan's phrase, "reorganize whole masses of life experience"; they convey issues in the large, and steer the psychic energies into new directions.

When we [the Diabasis community] were sometimes referred to as a "Laingian blow-out center," I balked, because there was some idealization of craziness in Laing's writings. At Diabasis we could not romanticize the process in this way, inasmuch as it represents a task of hard inner work and painstaking effort on the part of both staff and client. It would feel like a falsification to pretty up this picture and make it look light and easy, or somehow automatic. We were, however, on the basis of some years' experience with "severely psychotic" clients, optimistic about the process; after all, 85 percent of the clients in Diabasis I not only improved, with no medication, but most went on growing after leaving us.

IV

Dr. Burton: The concept of an alchemical vessel as the locus of behavior change is an apt one. Is this simply a metaphor or perhaps a structuralist concept of an actual therapeutic space which heals? In any event, do you feel the new "mix" comes out of these vessels because the monads or ingredients have been put in flux and must change their shape?

Dr. Perry: I feel, as Jung did, that the image of the vessel is nature's own expression of such a "therapeutic space." The metaphor is then not so much a *façon de parler* as it is an actual phenomenon, an affect-image that does work. The subjective experience of this image is that two individuals feel themselves sharing a center in common; this was perhaps more familiar to persons through psychedelic experiences, when one could do that, in which the sharing of a common center space could be an overwhelmingly vivid occurrence, packed with emotion and imagery of meaning.

I find the expression a "new mix" an apt one. A good therapist, as I see it, allows him/herself to be open enough to let go into a flux of this kind, and thus to allow him/herself to be modified by the experience of the other person's psyche. If there is to be real change, the client must be able to let go in the process, that is, to leave hold of the accustomed set and allow the psyche to do what it must. The consequent reordering or reintegrating is a change of shape in the sense that the structure of the psyche is altered by this complicated work of the affect-images.

V

Dr. Burton: You describe the renewal process of psychotherapy in the psychosis very well. Would you say that the principles of renewal apply as well to neurotic and characterological patients as they do to the psychotic, or perhaps with diminished intensity?

Dr. Perry: This renewal process does indeed take place in the therapy of many other kinds of personality besides the "schizophrenic." The essential factor is not the diagnostic category so much as the degree of depth to which the process goes, that is, the degree of activation of the archetypal affect-images, or the intensity as you suggest. It appears that in the "schizophrenic" acute episode, that is, the visionary state, the archetypal process is intensely energized and sped up, so that an entire process runs itself through in approximately six weeks typically. Forty days has become a number given sanctified recognition in a variety of traditions; one sees it in the historical accounts of mystics and prophets as well as in some techniques of altering consciousness, such as brainwashing. Therefore I am inclined to think that there may be a psychological principle determining this time span. Yet one may observe all the same contents and processes in persons who have a somewhat activated play of affect-images, only less overwhelming in strength and more strung out in time. There is in this a most intriguing question of the relation of time and intensity, apparently an inverse relation in which greater intensity varies together with diminished time.

My description of the therapeutic interaction in my paper is drawn from my regular practice with "normal neurotics," in which I spend three quarters of my time and which is largely composed of young professionals. Neurosis usually shows itself to be, as Jung has pointed out long since, a defensive cloaking of a growth process that is being warded off by too conventional and constricted a stance in respect to the new moves that strive in depth to occur and come to consciousness. When this propriety is relinquished, and the safer "common sense" or "professional" or "moral" safeguards are loosened, then this process in the affect-images becomes activated to seek a new orientation. In the "schizophrenic" episode, the relinquishing is no longer a matter of choice, since one's world-image and self-image fall apart automatically at the outset. Character problems present more difficulties, inasmuch as these habitual ways of deflecting what nature would otherwise prompt an individual to do are apt to be resistant to change; I believe that if such a character structure is to be altered at all, in anything more than the level of symptoms, it must involve the renewal process.

Appendix B
Setting Up a Residence Facility

In embarking upon this account of how to set up a residence facility for handling spiritual emergencies (i.e., the "extreme states of consciousness" formerly called schizophrenia), I must make an instant qualification. There is no one way, much less one right way. As I review in my mind the experiences of several such attempts made in the 1970s, Diabasis I and II in San Francisco, Soteria in San Jose, Prometheus in Fresno, Shadows in Nicasio, all in California, and Perry House in Las Vegas, New Mexico, one feature stands out clearly. Each time such a facility is brought to birth it is singular, different from all others, depending upon its parenthood. Each program is an expression of the outlook and preferences of its originators in respect to theory and method. I believe that this trait of facilities is only a special instance of a more general characteristic of the field of psychotherapy, that theory and method are recreated by each individual finding his or her own way in the field.

On the other hand, however, a facility needs to find and establish its identity, just as an individual does, and it requires a fairly firm consensus among the staff members as to its philosophy if there is to be a good working harmony among them. It is advisable to start with a small core group of originators, of perhaps three persons or so, who have the vision and initiative strongly enough to set the tone of the project.

From this point on I can do best by avoiding the handing out of directives and instead, making suggestions drawn from the experience of setting up three facilities in the 1970s, Diabasis I and II and Prometheus in Fresno, California.

There are advantages in selecting the staff at the beginning. Doing so gives the members the sense of creating the project together as a mutually shared responsibility rather than their being hired to work in an outfit already completed. There is an excitement in this creative endeavor that can be sustained throughout its further history.

How to make this selection for staffing was a question that baffled the three of us starting Diabasis; word got out about our notion without our making any public announcement, and fifty people were on the phone to apply—far too many to interview! So we cut the list in two and arranged to have twenty-five come to meet together in a group on each of two evenings. We sat on cushions in a circle with a jug of wine at its center and cups all around, and asked people to tell each other about themselves; each had about ten minutes. Personality inventories and profiles from tests were out of favor and intuitive impressions were trusted more. We were watching for certain traits: some previous experience of the inner life, whether through spiritual quests or crises, therapy, meditation, even psychedelic trips or peak experiences. We observed how they related in the group. Openness and respect for another person's differences were watched for, and the accompanying allowingness and tolerance. Warmth and caringness were of prime importance, as well as a readiness to express feelings. Interaction in a group brings out such qualities in bold relief. By the end of each evening, we felt we knew who would be most likely for this work, although we had to concede afterwards that the whole number were already self-selected by virtue of their interest in the venture and that we could have done well with any. There was a predominance of younger men and women, between their early twenties and late thirties, due perhaps to their outlook and cultural preferences deriving even indirectly from the large counterculture of the particular time and area. The advantage of these circumstances was that these young people were largely of the same age and subculture as the clients, and thus found a natural kinship with them.

The arithmetic of staffing, and perhaps also the geometry of the scheduling chart, are immensely complex. Some prefer the customary eight-hour shift for five days, but others need to have half the week off and therefore want twelve or even twenty-four hours on at a time. Weekends and holidays need special scheduling, of course, as well as certain days when the clients are more than usually active or disturbed. The number of staff is determined by these considerations, coming to at least twelve: three shifts of two each on weekdays and at least two shifts of two on weekends, with a couple more to cover for absenteeism. An administrative director (perhaps with a master of social work degree) and clinical director (psychiatrist or psychologist), and a secretary-finance person are also needed. When things are under way, a board of directors must be established for incorporation, and for this work the persons selected must truly understand and appreciate the philosophy of the project.

All this depends upon funding, needless to say and can be scaled upward or downward accordingly. Foundation grants are the obvious first recourse, but it must be borne in mind that such grants are almost always "seed-money," that is, coverage for the first two or three years of getting established enough to provide assurance that from that time on the project will be self-sustaining. A search for likely grantors can be best done at foundation councils or centers where former grant proposals and awards are recorded on microfilm, representing all the major transactions of recent decades. The printed catalogues listing the foundations and their policies are of less help since their descriptions are written principally for IRS approval and do not necessarily match the actual track record of awards. The proposal must be differently aimed each time for each particular foundation's interests. There are "How To" manuals explaining the proper format for a businesslike proposal, which should be a full and lengthy document starting with the project's philosophy, then specific methods, aims, and goals, the curriculum vitae of core staff—the originators—and a carefully elaborated budget. Other sources must also be approached, such as county funding for "general assistance," which provides for treatment or disability. One of the best ways of support beyond the initial years is to seek private funding from wealthy persons, each to sustain one bed throughout the year, with the promise of reports to the donor of all that happens to that bed's particular series of occupants; this could be highly motivating to some donors. Parents of psychotic offspring are also a likely source of funds.

Our preference at Diabasis was for a simple, homelike setting as noninstitutional as possible. We were introduced, through the considerate help of a colleague, to a kindly couple who had the wherewithal to purchase a building and give us its use at a low rental. The structure we selected was ideal, consisting of three levels of apartments and comprising twenty-two rooms; the living and dining rooms were wood-paneled and mellow with a fireplace in each. The warm atmosphere of these common spaces was just what we were seeking, and the Tudor facing of the front gave the assurance of the simplicity of style that would be found within.

At this point one applies for permits—an art in itself. In order to avoid stirring up alarm among the neighbors, we shunned any psychiatric definition of ourselves, which might raise difficult questions for permissible zoning; we called our work "reeducation for living for young adults"—hardly even a prevarication! The county codes customarily limit the number who can reside there to six. Exceeding that number involves a different category requiring a very costly hotel kitchen with a sloping floor and a sump in its midst, as well as an enclosed stairwell with metal doors, a design forbiddingly institutional and sure to break up the space into separated units. All the remodeling required consultation with inspectors from the building, fire, health, and zoning departments. One may count on taking on a great deal of legwork in the corridors of city hall.

Now things start to take shape, and the assigning of space establishes the entire space. It is advisable to have each of the six clients in his or her own single room. Bathrooms can be for both genders, without problems. The common room feels right with deep armchairs and sofa, supplemented with plenty of large cushions to sit or lie around on; the clients can gather before the fireplace to listen to music and read aloud or silently (often their own poetry, since creative expression abounds when given opportunity like this). High-spirited dancing also is a natural inclination for people in this mental space. The kitchen, opening into the dining room, turns out to be the preferred gathering place at all times of the day' and night. An art room for creative expression in various media is good for those who prefer to work at things alone, but many clients seem to prefer doing this out in the open on the dining table; thus the art room tends to become a supply room for materials of all kinds. A room or space apart from the bustle of activity is needed for meditation; the other kind of withdrawal, into one's preoccupations, usually tends to be done in one's bedroom, but with most it tends to drop away before long.

A rage room is a must, a specially equipped room with soft matting and padded sound-proofed walls. Whenever a client is feeling the impulse to let fly with anger or destructive impulses, he or she can do so in this place, with a punching bag (especially if life-size!), boffer swords, and cartons to smash up—but always in the presence of a staff member to whom the anger can be expressed and worked with. It is thus not at all a "seclusion room!"

The assigning of times now prepares for the actual work itself. As already mentioned, the scheduling of shifts is an on-going mathematical task of monstrous proportions, with all the individual preferences and requirements of some. It is advisable to have two persons, a male and a female, on at any part of the day and night, and a third available to help out if there is an unusual pitch of activity or disturbance. At Diabasis we set up a weekly three-hour conference of the total staff, mandatory for all so that everyone would be abreast of the newest developments; things move very fast in this kind of work. Otherwise we did not schedule programs and activities in a set way, since persons going through this experience are kept busy enough with their interior work. Whenever the time and circumstances felt right, however, there would be excursions to the beach or woods, or in-house gatherings for those who wanted guided dance- or body-movement exercises. Nor did we set times for retiring to bed or for rising; those who wanted to "sack out" during the morning were free to, and those who were inclined to be up at the middle of the night were free to, for that is the preferred time for persons in this mental state to be talkative or expressive of their inner process in various ways.

An item of scheduling that is awkward to accommodate, but necessary for the best functioning, is the weekly three-hour conference for the total staff membership, already mentioned. In Diabasis, at the staffs insistence, this meeting was only in part an occasion for acquainting everyone with the account of a new client or two, and only in part a discussion of how best to understand the psychology of some of the more critical moves in someone's process. Attention was principally focused less upon clients and more upon the personal experience that staff members might be undergoing in their work, whether it be puzzlement, frustration, anger, impatience, grief, or hurt. What was sought was not so much advice or "fixing it," as it was support and understanding on a very personal and feeling level. Staff could then learn much from each other. There were many moments that were deeply poignant and moving.

The chief vehicle in Diabasis for gaining an understanding of the psychology of clients and their process was a weekly consultation (sometimes called supervision) of each staff member with the professional therapist, in our case a psychiatrist, who was well acquainted with extreme states. These were individual sessions of an hour, sometimes for two staff persons together to augment the learning. In these, close scrutiny was given to a client's experience, tracking the inner process with its accompanying imagery and emotions.

The feeling was that the staff are the ones closest to the client hour by hour while things are proceeding rapidly from one part of the day to another in any person's process. Outside therapists are at a disadvantage in this respect. A more important point, though, is the question: What therapists know how to do this kind of work? Psychologists rarely come in contact with this kind of client, and psychiatrists have been groomed never to encourage any line of talk so "dereistic" as the "bizarre" ideation in this process. Anyone doing the work of tracking the inner process in the acute episode is approaching it newly, unprepared. Almost no psychological or psychiatric education trains one for this: such preparation provides one with little more than a generalized status of "qualification."

On these grounds, therefore, we started off with the assumption that all of us, professional and paraprofessional, were embarking upon a journey of learning and discovering from point zero. No one was considered expert and no one was boss. The staff were told in their second meeting that they were to be the creators of the facility rather than hired hands. The structure was democratic in the sense of being nonhierarchic. Each had the authority for the whole. Decisions and the making of policy were to come out of consensus of the entire staff. Agreement was to be attained not by vote but by acknowledging the "sense of the meeting," to use a term from the long-tried tradition of the Society of Friends. While this might appear cumbersome and time-consuming, it nevertheless promotes an increased consciousness of the issues involved. In place of a hierarchy of authority, we conceived ourselves to be a grouping of persons with particular skills leading to particular roles. In a moment of crisis, members represented the entire staff in the decisions they made, often instantaneously. This entire philosophy led to the happy eventuality that a high pitch of initiative was sustained by the whole staff—it was their show and they had a lively sense of pride in their creation. This was a far cry from having bosses and hired hands.

We did everything we could to make Diabasis a good place to be and spend time together. The staff was a group of unusually warm persons, who were affectionate and readily demonstrative of lovingness. Their manner with clients was to maintain a mutual openness with them so that the feeling of equality and of a nonauthoritarian way pertained not only to staff relations but included the client community. The result was that the feeling tone of the house, though perhaps at times subdued, was usually one of high spirits and jocular playfulness that was utterly spontaneous, never put on.

Therapy, if one may be allowed to call it that if it is conducted by paraprofessionals, was not the customary observer-style therapy, punctuated with interpretations. The therapeutic requirement was to support, encourage, and respond with empathetic feeling to the various expressions of the inner process. For this, it was felt that the best training was experience, learning from the interchange with an unbiased, open mind. For this work each client was assigned (or might choose) a "primary therapist" or sometimes a male and female pair instead, who would hold twice- or thrice-weekly sessions with him or her, in a room given to that purpose. Members each then had their own consultative interviews with a supervisor. The whole concept of therapy of this kind is based on the premise that the deep psyche does its own self-healing work in its own way, and that it needs a partner in the work, not a manager.

Since the renewal process tends to move very rapidly through its various phases in the acute episode, two months turned out to give plenty of time to undergo and assimilate it and so to prepare to move on. If that time span is set for all clients, it goes better than having an arbitrary length of stay, for the psyche adjusts itself to the time expectation. We offered a third month in another building for further assimilation and for efforts at "re-entry" into ordinary life settings, on a day-care plan, but the funding was withdrawn before this could be set up. Also, those who wanted were offered another six months of once-weekly interviews with the same primary therapist as before. With the two-month limit on residing full-time, we found the clients to be both ready to go by then and also eager to stay the full time up to that point, since it was experienced as a good place to be living.

We had no locked doors, and did not need them in the usual cases, although the occasional so-called schizoaffective conditions did present some real difficulties in containment, since their urge to run out was strong and heedless of promises to stay in. Other clients in the early stages sometimes had a somewhat customary urge to wander out, accompanied by a staff member; however, they usually returned very soon when they were dismayed to find that outside world to be "crazier" than anything within the house, and learned that it was not worth the adventure! Voluntary containment then came by a gradual learning process, and in this a feeling of loyalty to the community played a significant part.

Records were kept in inaccessible administrative rooms upstairs, off-limits to the clients, but on request one's records could be mediated and explained by one of the staff. Suicide precautions were not ordered for clients, because we felt that such alarm measures gave the wrong message—one of distrust in the client's own ability to handle the experience of the death image in an insightful way; suicide precautions convey the statement, "We expect you to try carrying that out." Our way worked well and without mishap.

In regard to management of the household, the clients and staff on their shift all ate together and cooked together, all in the interests of conviviality. We did have once-weekly help from a sweeper to do the more laborious housecleaning.

Legal liability is one of the most problematic issues in such a venture in these years of avaricious lawsuits for almost any occasion. The ultimate responsibility on such occasions rests with the board of directors, so that its members need to be kept constantly in touch with all unusual events that might lead to trouble of this nature, and for this they need the director of the project to be mediator between them and the staff. This need then eventuates in a hierarchical structure of responsibility different from the nature of the staff's own democratic-horizontal ways of governing themselves; much discussion and negotiating were required for this to become settled when legal threats arose for us. It is vitally necessary for the board members to have a direct, personal exposure to the manner in which issues are handled by the staff among themselves; perhaps visits at least to the staff conference would do, if spending time in the general community in operation would be too inconvenient. One item of legal concern is the use of carefully composed forms for "informed consent" upon admission, mandatory especially for a facility so deviant in its methods from the customary, generally approved practice.

In regard to finances, it has been determined, in our planning phase, that a residence facility of this kind is highly cost-effective. In the 1970s the cost per bed per day was a little under half that of hospital care; in the 1990s with the steeply rising cost of hospital stay it might well be found under a third. If one calculates the comparative costs of this care and the psychiatric ones over a five-year trajectory, calculating the highly expensive routines of later clinic visits and medical care and board-and-care arrangements, it can be demonstrated that this sort of facility can save the county large amounts of money.

To keep referrals coming in at a satisfactory pace (to avoid financial loss), the facility needs to make itself known to the therapeutic community and to the various agencies of the mental health system. It is imperative to try to maintain good will and mutual relatedness with the people composing that system. Fliers and newsletters are of great advantage in this effort.

In the process of starting up, it is a good plan to have the staff first meet together many times for entire evenings, if possible, to become related to each other on significant levels. They need to reveal themselves to each other with as much openness as they can, to learn not only to like each other but also to fight when that is called upon, to accept and to confront with ease. Through this the staff comes to feel quite like a large family whose members can do all of that with an underlying sense of belonging to each other. At the same time, much learning can go on as they discuss the philosophy and method of the project, and much creative thinking about how to do this work.

It is advisable to start taking admissions slowly and with cases not too complicated at the very first. One needs only to see the first example of someone being admitted in a state of full "insanity" and then becoming clear and coherent within a two or three days to find a gratifying enthusiasm lifting the energy. With all the pain in such crises, there is also even more joy in witnessing these transformations of personal development.

Appendix C
Alternatives to Hospitalization:
A Report on Diabasis

The concept of alternatives to hospitalization for acute episodes of "schizophrenia" was gaining ground in the 1970s, making its appearance in mental health budgets of states, counties, and foundations. Just what this term might actually imply and how such facilities might differ from hospitals had not yet become clear or agreed. Were they to provide a homelike atmosphere yet hold to the routine of medication, short-term admissions, and rapid turnover as in the customary crisis units? Was their aim the diversion of admissions from hospitals to avert their overload and avoid their high costs? How much were they expected to offer a different way of treatment in respect to psychotherapy, length of stay, and nonmedication?

The Facility

Diabasis was an experimental project in San Francisco that was addressing itself to these questions. It was a residence facility that lived through three years and more of inpatient work with acute "schizophrenic" episodes in young adults without the use of medications, always as part of the county's community mental health system. Its purpose was to provide a home in which the clients might have the opportunity to experience with full awareness their deepest processes during their intense turmoil. Since our permits only allowed six persons to sleep in the building, clients might stay up to two months as residents, but we added a third month to their care by a day program in which they must sleep elsewhere yet still participate in the same community. This device brought the number of clients under our daily care up to eight or nine at a time. We also provided a six-month follow-up in psychotherapy with the same staff members as before.

Staffing

The facility was staffed by twenty paraprofessionals who served not only the ordinary functions as attendants, but also provided psychotherapy as counselors. Some of these held fractions of our seven paid positions, while others were volunteers. Although this arrangement brought the secondary benefit of lower cost, its primary purpose lay in selecting individuals by disposition rather than by professional category; we picked ones who by qualities of empathy and ease with psychic depth were particularly suited to this work, whom we could then educate and train on the job. Student clinical placement was the source of much of our volunteer staffing. Two quarter-time psychiatrists supervised the work of psychotherapy in weekly individual interviews as well as in weekly staff conferences. The effect was that anxiety was kept at a low level and that a remarkable *savoir faire* had been developed by the members in this difficult work. The warm and dedicated spirit in which they worked was a major factor in making the project as successful as it was. Clients upon admission thus found themselves entering a vital and caring community of relationships.

In this way the staff remained open and involved without the burnout and self-protective closing-up that often occurs in this work. A measure of their enthusiasm was the fact that all paid staff stayed on for more than two years (one went on into researching the data), and even more volunteers have done the same. Gunderson has commented upon the effect of such staff attitudes upon outcome.[1]

Theory and Method

The orientation ultimately derived out of a Jungian[2] approach, though not all the staff were specifically given to that theory and method; instead, several modalities were drawn upon. There was a consensus on the basic viewpoint that the acute "psychotic" episode under discussion typically contains elements of a spontaneous reorganization of the self and that therefore, if it is handled well, may result in self-healing.[3] The therapeutic aim was to avoid the damage of labeling and disqualifying attitudes pointed out by Scheff[4] and instead, to respond to all that happens intrapsychically with honest feeling; also it was to validate the efforts the psyche makes spontaneously to effect a transition from a poor state of organization of the self to one that is more suited to the nature of the particular individual's disposition. The processes expressed in the imagery and emotion frequently lead to profound changes in one's outlook and lifestyle, specifically in one's cognitive structures, value system, and belief system.

In our attempt to define the parameters of our work, Larry Isaacs, a staff member, devised two innovative ways of viewing the "schizophrenic" episode: the "ideation category" and the "reality-oriented continuum":

> The ideation category presents certain thoughts that emerge during "schizophrenia." These thoughts are emotionally charged symbolic images of the psyche's need for transition. Powerful ideas of creation, birth, destruction, and death come to the fore. These ideas often become overwhelming to clients. The symbolic images which emerge demonstrate in a most extreme way the psychological direction that is needed to reorganize the psyche. Allowing this process to run its course, without imposing the usual restraints of dealing with "everyday realities," permits clients to find resolution to problems which initially seem unsolvable. Our descriptive data illustrates that there is quite often more than one ideational theme active in the "psychotic" process. The most common we have observed are feelings of death and birth or rebirth, world destruction and creation, clashes of ideological opposites, messianic calling; and supremacy of power, fears of being turned into the opposite sex also appear, as described by Perry.[5] If we were to consider the "ideation category" as the channel selector on a television set, selecting which area of concern the psyche is tuned to, the "reality-oriented continuum" would be the volume control to the set. It represents the intensity of the symbolic images which emerge from the psyche. In a full-blown "psychotic" process, the volume is on in the loud position. The client tends to identify or be possessed by these ideas, and there is little or no distinction from this inner content. If the volume is lower, as in the borderline psychotic process, the images become less consuming and the client has greater freedom to discriminate outside information from inner content.

A very large percentage of the clients we have served within the last year have undergone a highly active psychotic process. In it they have identified heavily with the symbolic images emerging from their psyche. Table C.1 shows the number of clients manifesting these features, under the headings "ideation" and "activity of psychotic process" (indicating the reality-oriented continuum).

Table C.1.

Descriptive Clinical Categories: 7/1/1977–2/28/1979

	All Clients	Acute Episodes
Ideational Themes		
Death	23	6
Opposites	31	11
Destruction	17	5
Creation	12	4
Regression	19	6
Birth	19	6
Messianic	25	9
Supremacy	25	11
Transsexual	10	3
Activity of Psychotic Process		
Active process	25	11
Borderline psychotic		
Unconscious predom.	9	4
Ego-conscious predom.	2	1
No psychotic process	9	0

Note: This table is based on the number of admissions in the period from July 1, 1977, to February 28, 1979: 30 males and 28 females, 58 in all; of these 18 were in acute episodes.

Whom We Served

Although our original design was to accept and serve selected cases of acute first episode, we soon found that we were not able to keep the house filled with these. We soon altered our criteria from acute first episodes to any episode marked by an acute activation of the unconscious psyche in terms of its process or content, that is, mythic imagery, delusions, hallucinations, and so on. Since we had difficulty receiving referrals in sufficient number, we made ourselves available to clients in a wide range of conditions. A similarly broad range of economic status was made possible by funding of four out of the six beds from the county mental health budget, the rest paying privately. The distribution of cases reflected these changes, such that only one case in three was in an acute episode, of which less than half were first episodes. Many have turned out to be manic or depressive, and several have been chronic.

Robert Schwartz has assembled the following data:

In twenty-eight months, July 1, 1977 to November 1, 1979, we admitted 84 cases. Of this number we have made a simple demographic study of the first twenty months with its 58 cases. Since our ceiling on time was two months, it is evident that most clients made use of their full time, i.e., 36 per year. The majority of these 58 clients were white, 18-29 years old, and single. At least half of the client population had 13-15 years education. The number of women grew from roughly one half to two thirds during these two years. The psychiatric history shows that almost all of the clients were referred to us by private therapists or psychiatric hospitals. The majority of our clients had been hospitalized at least once prior to admission. Almost all of these had experienced phenothiazines prior to admission. The average length of stay for all clients has been 48 days (private one 51.3, county one 43.7).

Further tabulations of data appear in tables C.2 and C.3.

TABLE C.2

Diagnostic Categories: 7/1/1977–2/28/1979

Systems	All Clients	Acute Schizophrenic Episodes
DSM II Final Diagnosis		
295.4	18	18
296.9	7	0
295.74	6	0
295.73	5	0
307.3	4	0
301.2	2	0
Other	16	0
Global Assessment Scale		
Upon Admission		
1-10	0	0
11-20	3	3
21-30	16	3
31-40	14	6
41-50	14	2
51-60	10	4
61-70	1	0
71-80	0	0
81-90	0	0
91-100	0	0

TABLE C.3

Client Data: 7/1/1977–2/28/1979

Information	All Clients	Acute Schizophrenic Episodes
Length of Stay		
1-7 days	10	5
8-14 days	7	0
15-21 days	6	1
22-28 days	3	2
29-35 days	2	0
36-42 days	3	2
43-49 days	2	1
50-56 days	2	0
more than 56 days	23	7
Referral Source		
Private physician	2	1
Private therapist	17	6
Hospital	24	6
Friends	5	1
Relatives	8	2
Self	2	2
Other	0	0
Previous Hospitalization		
None	17	7
1	19	7
2	12	4
3 or more	5	0
Medication History		
Phenothiazines	34	8
Minor Tranquilizers	2	0
Lithium	0	0
Antidepressants	0	0
Other	1	0

Progress of Therapy

Our most surprising finding in the cases of early acute episode was that grossly "psychotic" clients have usually come into a coherent and reality-oriented state spontaneously within two to six days, without need for medications. We have found that our work was most effective with those acute early episodes that were productive of imageful content. With clients who came to us in their third or fourth episode, we often found that their experience was beneficial but the outcome less striking. Chronicity was another matter and the chances of fruitful experiences more uncertain. A history of heavy medication usually made it difficult to do effective psychotherapeutic work.

To our great regret, Diabasis was closed in November 1979 because of cutbacks in the county's mental health budget. We were well enough regarded to be asked to remain as part of the mental health system; however, the only place for us on its flowchart was as a "hospital divergence facility" with the limit of an eight-day stay, essentially as a money-saving device. This service would have been so restricted that we could not see ourselves providing it. A similar fate befell a facility in New Mexico, Perry House in Las Vegas, which operated on the same model for two years with comparably fine results.[6]

Conclusions

Returning to the question of what alternative programs can be, we arrived at certain conclusions. Such a program can be much more than benign milieu therapy. It is possible to do effective psychotherapy in the acute episode, since the client's talk is clear and the material of dynamics active and ready to hand. The use of medications can be reserved for backup alone, for the rare times when behavior becomes hard to handle, and after other psychological means have been attempted. Therapy is best conducted in the spirit of a nondoctrinaire openness to learn from the clients what the experience of their altered states is, and what it feels like to go through this process, and thus to be of help in facilitating its own aims toward reorganizing the self. When allowed to proceed, we find that a growth process is often under way that can be sustained, with consequent developments in one's system of meanings, values, beliefs, and lifestyle. This treatment mode may then help avoid the devastating picture of incapacitation and recidivism that now prevails, and then becomes a burden to mental health systems. The cost-effectiveness of such a program depends entirely upon its use by the community to handle acute and early, if not first, episodes, with the prospect that these clients might be benefited in such a way that they would no longer remain indigents, dependent upon the county for aftercare.

We therefore point to the advantages gained if a low-cost residence facility were to be placed in each mental health district as an alternative to hospitalization for the promising acute cases, especially in cities that can draw upon graduate student populations for staffing.

Notes

Introduction

1. J. W. Perry, *The Self in Psychotic Process* (Berkeley: University of California Press, 1953; reprinted Dallas: Spring Publications, 1987).

2. J. W. Perry, *Roots of Renewal in Myth and Madness* (San Francisco: Jossey-Bass, 1976).

Chapter 1. Treatment or Therapy?

1. Liddell and Scott, *An Intermediate Greek-English Lexicon* (New York: American Book), 362.

2. E. Jantsch, *The Self-Organizing Universe* (Oxford and New York: Pergamon Press, 1980); I. Prigogine, *Order Out of Chaos: Man's New Dialogue with Nature* (New York: Bantam Books, 1984); J. Gleik, *Chaos: Making a New Science* (New York: Viking Penguin, 1987).

3. H. F. Dunbar, *Emotions and Bodily Changes* (New York: Columbia University Press, 1936).

4. G. L. Engel, "The Clinical Application of the Biopsychosocial Model," *American Journal of Psychiatry* 137 5 (1981): 535–44.

5. R. D. Laing and A. Esterson, *Sanity, Madness and the Family* (Baltimore: Pelican Books, 1970).

6. R. W. Leeper, "Motivational Theory of Emotion to Replace Emotion as Disorganizational Response," *Psychological Review* 55. 1 (January 1948): 5–21.

7. A. Ellis, *Growth through Reason* (Palo Alto, Calif.: Science and Behavior Books, 1971).

8. R. A. Fischer, "A Cartography of the Ecstatic and Meditative States," *Science* 124 (November 26, 1971): 897–904.

9. E. Bleuler, *Dementia Praecox or the Group of Schizophrenias*, trans. J. Zinkin, (New York: International University Press, 1950).

10. Jung, C. G. *The Secret of the Golden Flower*, Trans. C. F. Baynes (London: Kegan Paul, Trench and Trubner, 1935), 116–18.

11. J. Locke, "Essay Concerning Human Understanding," in *Philosophical Works* (London: St. John, Ed., 1854).

12. S. Arieti, *Interpretation of Schizophrenia* (New York: Robert Brunner, 1955), 191–92.

13. K. Dabrowski, *Postive Disintegration* (Boston: Little, Brown, 1986).

14. M. Rappaport et al., "Are There Schizophrenics for Whom Drugs May be Unnecessary or Contraindicated?" *International Pharmacopsychiatry* 13 (1978): 100–111.

15. L. R. Mosher and A. Z. Menn, "Community Residential Treatment for Schizophrenia: 2 Year Followup," *Hospital and Community Psychiatry* 29 (1978): 715–23.

16. II Esdras, ch. XIV *The Aprocrypha*, ed. M. Komroff (New York: Tudor, 1936).

17. Matthew 4:1–2, in *The Dartmouth Bible*, R. B. Chamberlin, et al. (Boston: Houghton Mifflin, 1961).

18. A. Dundes, *The Flood Myth* (Berkeley: University of California Press, 1988).

19. A. T. Boisen, *The Exploration of the Inner World* (Chicago: Willett Clark & Co., 1936).

Chapter 2. Thought Disorder

1. P. A. Sorokin, *The Crisis of Our Age* (New York: Dutton, 1942).

2. C. G. Jung, *Two Essays on Analytical Psychology*, trans. R. F. C. Hull, in *Collected Works*, vol. 7, Bollingen Series XX (Princeton, N.J.: Princeton University Press, 1959).

3. J. R. Morrison, "Changes in Subtypes of Schizophrenia, 1920–66," *American Journal of Psychiatry* 131 (June 1974): 674–7.

4. J. B. Rhine, *Extra-sensory Perception* (Boston, 1934).

5. J. S. Kasanin, "The Disturbance of Conceptual Thinking in Schizophrenia," in *Language and Thought in Schizophrenia*, ed. J. S. Kasanin (Berkeley: University of California Press, 1944), 89.

6. K. Goldstein, "Methodological Approach to The Study of Schizophrenic Thought Disorder," in *Language and Thought in Schizophrenia*.

7. L. Vitgotsky, "Thought in Schizophrenia," *Archives of Neurology and Psychiatry* 31 (1934): 1063.

8. J. S. Kasanin, *Language and Thought in Schizophrenia.*

9. A. Storch, "The Primitive and Archaic Forms of Inner Experience and Thought in Schizophrenia," *Journal of Nervous and Mental Diseases,* Monograph Series No. 36, 1924.

10. R. A. Fischer, "A Cartography of the Ecstatic and Meditative States," *Science* 174 (November 26, 1971): 897–904.

11. N. Cameron, "Experimental Analysis of Schizophrenic Thinking," in J. S. Kasanin, *Language and Thought in Schizophrenia,* 55.

12. S. P. Zarlock, "Societal Expectations, Language and Schizophrenia," *Journal of Humanistic Psychology* (Spring, 1966): 68–74.

13. H. S. Sullivan, "The Language in Schizophrenia" in J. S. Kasanin, *Language and Thought in Schizophrenia.*

14. S. Arieti, *Interpretation of Schizophrenia* (New York: Robert Brunner, 1935), ch. 10.

Chapter 3. Psychosis or Visionary State?

1. K. Dabrowski, *Positive Disintegration* (Boston: Little Brown, 1966).

2. C. G. Jung, "Mind and Earth," (1931), in *Civilization in Transition, Collected Works,* vol. 10, Bollingen Series XX (Princeton, N.J.: Princeton University Press, 1959).

3. M. Rappaport et al., "Are There Schizophrenics for Whom Drugs May Be Unnecessary or Contraindicated?" *International Pharmacopsychiatry* 13 (1978): 100–111.

4. J. W. Perry, *Lord of the Four Quarters* (New York: Paulist Press, 1991; orig. published 1966).

5. J. W. Perry, *The Heart of History* (Albany: State University of New York Press, 1987).

6. K. S. Latourette, *The Chinese: Their History and Culture* (New York: Macmillan, 1946); C. P. Fitzgerald, *China* (New York: Praeger, 1961).

7. A. F. C. Wallace, *The Death and Rebirth of the Seneca* (New York: Knopf, 1970).

8. V. Lantemari, *The Religions of the Oppressed* (New York: Mentor Books. New American Library, 1965).

9. T. J. Scheff, *Being Mentally Ill* (Chicago: Aldine, 1966).

10. E. H. Erickson, *Insight and Responsibility* (New York: Norton, 1964).

Chapter 4. Alternative Ways

1. L. R. Mosher and A. Menn, "Lowered Barriers in the Community: The Soteria Model," in *Alternative to Mental Hospital Treatment*, ed. L. A. Stein and M. A. Test (New York: Plenum Press, 1979), 75–113.

2. J. W. Perry, "Reconstitutive Process in the Psychopathology of the Self," *Annals of the New York Academy of Sciences* 96, Art. 3 (January 27, 1962): 8553–76.

3. A. M. Boisen, *The Exploration of the Inner World* (New York: Willet Clark, 1936), 43–47, 52–57.

4. R. P. Liberman, J. H. Fallon, and C. J. Wallace, "Drug-Psychosocial Interactions in the Treatment of Schizophrenia," 1984 in *The Chronically Mentaly Ill: Research and Services*, ed. M. Mirabi (New York: Spectrum Publications, 1984); W. T. Carpenter and D. W. Heinrichs, "Treatment-Relevant Subtypes in Schizophrenia," *Journal of Nervous and Mental Disease* 169.2 (1981): 113–19.

5. M. Rappaport et al., "Are There Schizophrenics for Whom Drugs May Be Unnecessary or Contraindicated?" *International Pharmacopsychiatry* 13 (1978): 100–111.

6. J. G. Gunderson, "Drugs and Psychosocial Treatment of Schizophrenia Revisited," *Journal of Continuing Medical Education* (December 1977): 25–40.

7. L. R. Mosher, R. J. Wendt, S. M. Mathews, and A. Z. Menn, "Comparison of Two Environments for Schizophrenia," in *Principles and Practice of Milieu Therapy*, ed. J. G. Gunderson, O. A. Will, Jr., and L. Mosher (New York: Jason Aronson, 1983), 117–33.

8. C. Rogers, *Client-Centered Therapy in Current Practice: Implications and Theory* (Boston: Houghton Mifflin, 1951).

9. H. I. Levene, "Acute Schizophrenia: Clinical Effects of The Labelling Process," *Archives of General Psychiatry* 25 (September 1971): 215–22.

10. J. W. Perry, *The Far Side of Madness* (Dallas: Spring Publications, 1989; orig. published 1974), ch. 12.

11. E. Bleuler, *Dementia Praecox or the Group of Schizophrenias* (New York: International Universities Press, 1950).

12. R. D. Laing, and A. Esterson, *Sanity, Madness and the Family* (Baltimore: Pelican Books, 1970).

13. T. J. Scheff, *Being Mentally Ill* (Chicago: Aldine, 1960).

14. A. van. Gennep, *The Rites of Passage* (Chicago: Aldine, 1966).

15. R. A. Fischer, "A Cartography of the Ecstatic and Meditative States," *Science* 174 (November 26, 1971): 897–904.

16. E. H. Erickson, *Insight and Responsibility* (New York: Norton, 1964).

Chapter 5. Transitions in Outlook

1. M. Eliade, *The Myth of the Eternal Return*, trans. W. R. Trask, Bollingen Series XLVI (New York: Pantheon, 1954).

2. J. W. Perry, *Lord of the Four Quarters* (New York: Paulist Press, 1991; orig. published 1966).

3. J. W. Perry, *Roots of Renewal in Myth and Madness* (San Francisco: Jossey-Bass, 1976).

4. V. G. Childe, *New Light on the Most Ancient East* (New York: Grove Press, 1987).

5. J. W. Perry, *The Heart of History* (Albany: State University of New York Press, 1987).

6. Ibid.

7. J. Lame Deer, *Lame Deer, Seeker of Visions*, ed. R. E. Erdoes (New York: Washington Square Press, 1976).

8. P. Worsley, *The Trumpet Shall Sound: A Study of the Cargo Cults of Melanesia* (London: 1957); V. Lanternari, *Religions of the Oppressed* (New York: Mentor Books, New American Library, 1965).

9. A. F. C. Wallace, "Stress and Rapid Personality Change," *International Record of Medicine and General Practice Clinics* 169.12 (1956); idem, *Culture and Personality* (New York: Random House, 1961).

10. W. La Barre, "Materials for a History of Studies of Crisis Cults: A Bibliographical Essay," *Current Anthropology* 12.1 (1971).

11. Perry, *The Heart of History*.

Chapter 6. Psychological Methods

1. J. W. Perry, *Roots of Renewal in Myth and Madness* (San Francisco: Jossey-Bass, 1976), appendix.

2. A. Dundes, *The Flood Myth* (Berkeley: University of California Press, 1988).

3. W. B. Yeats, *The Winding Stair and Other Poems* (New York: Macmillan, 1933).

4. M. Eliade, *Myth and Reality*, trans. W. R. Trask (New York: Harper & Row, 1963), ch. 4.

5. W. A. White, The Language in Schizophrenia," *Schizophrenia* (New York: Hoeber, 1928).

6. J. Silverman, "The Problem of Attention in Research and Theory in Schizophrenia," *Psychological Review* 71 (1964): 352–79.

7. J. Silverman, "Personality Trait and 'Perceptual Style': Studies of the Psychotherapists of Schizophrenic Patients," *Journal of Nervous and Mental Diseases* 145 (1967): 5–17.

8. R. Otto, *The Idea of the Holy* (London: Oxford University Press, 1950).

9. Psalm 23 in *The Dartmouth Bible*, ed. Chamberlin et al. (Boston: Houghton Mifflin, 1961).

10. J. W. Perry, *The Self in Psychotic Process* (Dallas, Spring Publications, 1987; orig. published 1954), appendix, Case Protocols.

11. J. W. Perry, *Roots of Renewal in Myth and Madness*, ch. 5, sec. 7.

12. C. G. Jung, "Studies in Word Association" (1905–9), in *Experimental Researches*, trans. R. F. C. Hull, *Collected Works*, vol. 2, Bollingen Series XX (Princeton, N.J.: Princeton University Press, 1965).

13. A. W. E. O'Shaughnessy, "Ode," in *The Oxford Book of English Verse*, ed. A. T,. Quiller-Couch (Oxford: Clarendon Press, 1905), 828.

14. John 20:11–13, in *The Dartmouth Bible*, 1184–85.

15. John 22:1–2, in *The Dartmouth Bible*, 1185.

Chapter 7. Jung's Approach

1. T. Roszak, *Where the Wasteland Ends* (Garden City: Doubleday, 1972).

2. C. G. Jung, "The Psychology of Dementia Praecox" (1907), in *The Psychogenesis of Mental Disease*, trans. R. F. C. Hull, *Collected Works*, vol 3, Bollingen Series XX (Princeton, N.J.: Princeton University Press, 1957); idem, *Symbols of Transformation*, trans. R. F. C. Hull, *Collected Works*, vol. 5, Bollingen Series XX (Princeton, N.J.: Princeton University Press, 1956).

3. J. W. Perry, *The Heart of History* (Albany: State University of New York Press, 1987).

4. C. G. Jung, *Psychology and Alchemy*, trans. R. F. C. Hull, *Collected Works*, vol. 12, Bollingen Series XX (Princeton, N.J.: Princeton University Press, 1955).

5. Roszak, *Where the Wasteland Ends*.

6. Ibid.

7. Ibid., 294. (Concerning the mathematical analysis of nature—the highest espression of objectivity in science): "But how did Descartes happen upon this momentous insight? The story we have from Descartes himself is that in November of 1619, an angel descended upon him in three dream-visions and revealed the possibilities of a marvelous new mathematical science. This, Descartes decided, was surely the angel of truth, and with its inspiration he devised the analytical geometry." This is recounted in Laurence J. Lafleur's introduction, to Descartes' *Philosophical Essays*, (N.Y., Library of Liberal Arts, 1964).

8. Ibid., 281.

9. Ibid., 331

10. Ibid., 332.

11. C. G. Jung, "Two Kinds of Thinking," in *Symbols of Transformation*.

12. R. E. Ornstein, *The Psychology of Consciousness* (San Francisco: Freeman, 1972).

13. C. G. Jung, "On Psychological Understanding" (1914), in *The Psychogenesis of Mental Disease*, ch. 3

14. C. G. Jung, "On Psychic Energy," in *The Structure and Dvnamics of The Psyche* (1948), trans. R. F. C. Hull, *Collected Works*, vol. 8, Bollingen Series XX (Princeton, N.J.: Princeton University Press, 1965).

15. Jung, "On Psychological Understanding."

16. E. Kris, *Psychoanalytic Explorations in Art* (New York: International Universities Press, 1952).

17. C. G. Jung, "The Transcedent Function" (1916–58), in *The Structure and Dynamics of the Psyche*.

18. Jung, "On Psychological Understanding."

19. Ibid., 191.

20. C. G. Jung, "The Content of the Psychoses" (1914), "On the Importance of the Unconscious in Psychopathology" (1914), and "On the Problem of Psychogenesis in Mental Disease" (1919), in *The Psychogenesis of Mental Disease*.

21. C. G. Jung, *Symbols of Transformation*, trans. R. F. C. Hull, *Collected Works*, vol. 5, Bollingen Series XX (Princeton, N.J.: Princeton University Press, 1956).

Chapter 9. Love and Power

1. C. G. Jung, "Commentary on the Secret of the Golden Flower" (1929), in *Alchemical Studies*, trans. R. F. C. Hull, *Collected Works*, vol. 13, Bollingen Series XX. (Princeton, N.J.: Princeton University Press, 1973).

2. T. Roszak, *Where the Wasteland Ends* (Garden City, N.Y.: Doubleday, 1972).

3. J. W. Perry, "Eros and History," *Anima* 3.1 (1976): 30–38.

4. J. Needham, *Time: The Refreshing River* (London: Allen and Unwin, 1943).

5. Teilhard de Chardin, *The Phenomenon of Man* (New York: Harper and Row, 1965).

6. A. F. C. Wallace, *Culture and Personality* (New York: Random House, 1970).

7. J. W. Perry, *Lord of the Four Quarters* (New York: Braziller, 1966; New York: Paulist Press, 1991).

8. Perry, *Lord of the Four Quarters*; H. Frankfort, *Kingship and the Gods.* (Chicago: University of Chicago Press, 1948).

9. W. LaBarre, "Materials for History of Studies of Crisis Cults: A Bibliographic Essay," *Current Anthropology* 12.1 (1971): 3–44; A. F. C. Wallace, "Stress and Rapid Personality Change," *International Record of Medical and General Practice Clinics* 169.12, (1956): 761–74.

10. V. G. Childe, *The Prehistory of European Society* (London: Penguin, 1954).

11. Frankfort, *Kingship and the Gods*, ch. 12.

12. A. Bentzen, *King and Messiah* (London: Butterworth, 1955).

13. Y. L. Fung, *A Short History of Chinese Philosophy*, trans. D. Bodde (New York: Macmillan, 1960).

14. Mencius, *The Work of Mencius*, in *The Four Books*, ed. J. Legge (Shanghai: The Commercial Press, 1934).

15. Mo-tse, "Mo-tse," trans. Y. P. Mei, in *The Wisdom of China and Indian*, ed. Lin Yu-tang (New York: Random House, 1942).

16. Chuang-tse, "The Writings of Chuang-Tse," in *The Texts of Taoism*, ed. J. Legge (New York: Julian Press, 1959).

17. E. J. Thomas, *The Life of Buddha as Legend and History*, quoting the "Lalita-vistara" (New York: Barnes and Noble, 1960).

18. D. Bodde, "Harmony and Conflict in Chinese Philosophy," in *Studies and Thought in Chinese Philosophy*, A. Wright (Chicago: University of Chicago Press, 1953).

19. Perry, *Roots of Renewal in Myth and Madness*, ch. 6.

20. S. Mowinckel, *He That Cometh*, trans. G. W. Anderson (New York: Abingdon, 1954), ch. 6.

21. J. Klausner, *The Messianic Idea in Isreal*, trans. F. W. Steinspring (New York: Macmillan, 1955).

22. I Enoch, *Book of Enoch*, from "The Apocrypha and Psuedepigrapha of the Old Testament," ed. R. H. Charles (Oxford: Clarendon Press, 1913), vol. II, 163–281, republished by Work of the Chariot 3, 1970.

23. T. H. Gaster, *The Dead Sea Scriptures* (Garden City, N.Y.: Doubleday Anchor Books, 1956).

24. J. W. Perry, *The Self in Psychotic Process* (Berkeley: University of California Press, 1953; Dallas: Spring Publications, 1987).

25. Perry, *The Far Side of Madness*, ch. 7.

26. R. E. Ornstein, *The Psychology of Consciousness* (San Francisco: W. H. Freeman, 1972).

27. A. Deikman, "Bimodal Consciousness," *Archives for General Psychiatry* 45 (1971): 481–89.

28. R. Fischer, "A Cartography of the Ecstatic and Meditative States," *Science* 174 (1971): 897–904.

29. M. Foucault, *Madness and Civilization* (New York: New American Library, Mentor Books, 1967).

Chapter 10. Individuality

1. V. G. Childe, *New Light on the Most Ancient East* (New York: Evergreen Books, Grove Press, 1947).

2. J. W. Perry, *Lord of the Four Quarters* (New York: Paulist Press, 1991; orig. published 1966).

3. J. W. Perry, *Roots of Renewal in Myth and Madness* (San Francisco: Jossey-Bass, 1976).

4. J. Needham, "Human Laws and Laws of Nature in China and the West," *Journal of the History of Ideas* 12 (1951): 250.

5. H. G. Creel, *The Birth of China* (New York: Frederick Ungar, 1937) 182–84.

6. Ibid., 342–43.

7. Tung Chung-Shu, "Ch'ien ch'u fan-lu," sec. 43, trans. B. Watson, in "The Imperial Age: Ch'in and Hu," *Sources of Chinese Tradition*, part II, Ed. W. T. de Bary (New York: Columbia University Press, 1960).

8. K. C. Chang, *Art, Myth and Ritual* (Cambridge: Harvard University Press, 1983); P. Wheatley, *The Pivot of the Four Quarters* (Chicago: Alden, 1971).

9. S. v. R. Cammann, "Suggested Orgins of the Tibetan Mandala Painting," *Art Quarterly* vol. 13. no. 2 (Spring 1950): 106–119.

10. W. E. Soothill, *The Hall of Light: A Study of Early Chinese Kingship* (New York: Philosophical Library, 1952).

11. Chang, *Art, Myth and Ritual*, ch. 3.

12. J. W. Perry, *The Heart of History* (Albany: State University of New York Press, 1987), chs. 4 and 5.

13. J. H. Breasted, *The Dawn of Conscience*, (New York: Charles Scribner, 1983).

14. Creel, *The Birth of China*.

15. Confucius, *Analects* VI.22.1, in *The Analects of Confucius*, trans. A. Waley (New York: Vintage Books, Random House, 1938).

16. Mencius, *The Four Books*, trans. J. Legge (Shanghai: The Commercial Press).

17. Mo-Tse, in *The Wisdom of the East*, ed. Lin Yu-Tang (New York: Random House, 1942), 385ff.

18. A. Waley, *The Way and Its Power* (New York: Grove Press, 1958).

Chapter 11. Healing

1. D. Sandner, *Navaho Symbols of Healing* (New York: Harvest Books, Harcourt Brace and Jovanovich, 1979); F. Waters, *The Masked Gods: Navaho and Pueblo Ceremonialism* (New York: Ballantine Books, 1950).

2. J. W. Perry, *Roots of Renewal in Myth and Madness* (San Franscisco: Jossey-Bass, 1976), appendix, Case Protocols.

3. M. Eliade, *The Myth of the Eternal Return*, trans. W. R. Trask, Bollingen Series XLVI (New York: Pantheon, 1954).

4. Perry, *Roots of Renewal*, ch. 5.

5. Eliade, *The Myth of the Eternal Return*, ch. 2.

6. M. Eliade, *Myth and Reality*, trans. W. R. Trask (New York: Harper & Row, 1963), 30.

7. V. G. Childe, *New Light on the Most Ancient East* (New York: Grove Press, 1957).

8. Eliade, *Myth and Reality*.

9. Ibid., 33.

10. Ibid., 30–31.

11. Ibid., 24–25.

12. A. F. C. Wallace, "Stress and Rapid Personality Change," *International Record of Medicine and General Practice Clinics* 169.12 (1956).

13. V. Lanternari, *The Religions of the Oppressed* (New York: Mentor Books, New American Library, 1965).

14. Lame Deer, *Lame Deer, Seeker of Visions*, ed. R. Erdoes (New York: Washington Square Press, 1976).

15. K. Ring, *Life at Death* (New York: Quill, Morrow, 1982), 83.

16. K. Ring, "Prophetic Visions in 1988: A Critical Reappraisal," *Journal of Near-Death Studies* 7 (1988): 4–18.

17. C. G. Jung, *Psychology and Alchemy*, trans. R. F. C. Hull, *Collected Works*, vol. 12, Bollingen Series XX (Princeton, N.J.: Princeton University Press, 1965).

18. Ibid., 235, 259, 261, 321; C. G. Jung, *Mysterium Coniunctionis*, trans. R. F. C. Hull, *Collected Works*, vol. 14, Bollingen Series XX (Princeton, N.J.: Princeton University Press, 1965), 339.

19. J. W. Perry, *The Heart of History* (Albany: State University of New York Press, 1987).

20. L. Dossey, *Space, Time and Medicine* (Boulder, Colo.: Shambhala, 1982).

21. Ibid., 48.

22. Ibid., 168.

23. Ibid., 21.

24. I. Prigogine, *Order Out of Chaos: Man's New Dialogue with Nature* (New York: Bantam Books, 1984).

25. E. Jantsch, *The Self-Organizing Universe* (Oxford and New York: Pergamon Press, 1980).

26. M. Ferguson, *The Aquarian Conspiracy* (Los Angeles: Tarcher, 1980), 165–66.

27. Dossey, *Time, Space and Medicine*, 176.

28. Ibid., 200.

29. N. J. Girardot, "Behaving Cosmologically in Early Taoism," in *Cosmogony and Ethical Order*, ed. R. Lovin and F. E. Reynolds (Chicago: University of Chicago Press, 1975).

30. J. Schwartz and M. McGuiness, *Einstein for Beginners* (New York: Pantheon, 1979), 82.

31. Dossey, *Space, Time and Medicine*, 42.

32. H. Hesse, "Incipit Vita Nuova," in *Stories of Five Decades*, trans. R. Manheim, ed. T. Ziolkowski (London: Triad/Panther, 1976), 41–42.

Chapter 12. Visionary Experience

1. Plato, *Phaedrus*, in *The Dialogues of Plato*, trans. B. Jowett (Oxford: Clarendon Press, 1871), 578–79.

2. P. B. Shelley, "Prometheus Unbound," in *The Poetical Works of Percey Bysshe Shelley*, ed. Mary Shelley (London: Edward Maxon, 1857).

3. P. B. Shelley, "Masque of Anarchy," in *The Poetical Works*, LXXX, LXXXV, LXXXVI, XC, XCII, pp. 372–74.

4. T. Webb, *Shelley: A Voice Not Understood* (Mancester, U.K.: Manchester University Press, 1977), 124 and 147.

5. Mary Shelley, "Notes on Prometheus Unbound," in P. B. Shelley, *The Poetical Works*, 367–68.

6. P. B. Shelley, *The Poetical Works*, 303

7. Ibid., 323.

8. Ibid., 354–55.

9. Ibid., 355.

10. Ibid., 357.

11. Maenads were frenzied women in Dionysian rites. Agave was a maenad, mother of the sacrificed Pentheus.

12. Shelley, *The Poetical Works*, 362.

13. F. Barron, *Creativity and Psychological Health* (Princeton, N.J.: Van Nostrand, 1963), 243–47.

14. Ibid.

15. R. A. Fischer, "A Cartography of the Ecstatic and Meditative States," *Science* 174 (November 26, 1971): 897–904.

16. A. H. Maslow, *The Farther Reaches of Human Nature* (New York: Viking, 1971), ch. 4.

17. A. F. C. Wallace, *Culture and Personality* (New York: Random House, 1970).

18. H. R. E. Davidson, *Gods and Myths of Northern Europe* (Baltimore: Penguin, 1964), ch. 8; E. O. G. Turneville-Petre, *Myth and Religion of the North* (New York: Holt, Rhinehart and Wilson, 1964).

19. A. Danielou, *Shiva and Dionysus*, trans. K. F. Hurry (New York: Inner Traditions International, 1984).

20. Davidson, *Gods and Myths of Northern Europe*, 70.

21. Ibid.

22. C. Kerenyi, *Dionysus*, Bollingen Series LXV, vol. 2 (Princeton, N.J.: Princeton University Press, 1975).

23. Turneville-Petre, *Myth and Religion of the North*, 37–38.

24. Ibid., 42.

25. W. F. Otto, *Dionysus: Myth and Cult*, trans. P. B. Palmer (Bloomington: Indiana University Press, 1965), ch. 11.

26. K. Ring, *Life at Death* (New York: Quill, Morrow, 1982).

27. K. Ring, *Heading toward Omega* (New York: Quill, Morrow, 1984), 83.

28. J. W. Perry, *Roots of Renewal in Myth and Madness* (San Francisco: Jossey-Bass, 1976), Appendix, Case Protocols.

Summary

1. C. G. Jung, "Schizophrenia," in *The Psychogenesis of Mental Disease*, trans, R. F. C. Hull, *Collected Works*, vol. 3, Bollingen Series XX (Princeton, N.J.: Princeton University Press, 1959).

2. John, Gospel 3:8. in *The Dartmouth Bible* (Boston: Houghton Mifflin, 1961).

3. J. W. Perry, *The Self in Psychotic Process* (Berkeley: University of California Press, 1953; Dallas: Spring Publications, 1987); idem, *The Far Side of Madness* (Englewood Cliffs, N.J.: Prentice Hall, 1974; Dallas, Spring Publications, 1989); *Roots of Renewal in Myth and Madness* (San Francisco: Jossey-Bass, 1976).

4. A. F. C. Wallace, *Culture and Personality* (New York: Random House, 1961); V. Lanternari, *Religions of the Oppressed* (New York: Mentor Books, New American Library, 1965).

5. J. W. Perry, "Emotions and Object Relations," *Journal of Analytical Psychology* 15.1 (1970): 1–12.

6. Perry, *The Self in Psychotic Process*.

7. J. W. Perry, *The Heart of History* (Albany: State University of New York Press, 1987).

8. S. Grof, *Realms of the Human Unconscious: Observations from L.S.D. Research* (New York: E. P. Dutton, 1976); idem, *Beyond the Brain: Birth, Death and Transcendence in Psychotherapy* (Albany: State University of New York Press, 1985).

9. Paul, Hebrews 10:31.

10. L. R. Mosher and A. Menn, "Lowered Barriers in the Community: The Soteria Model," in *Alternatives to Mental Hospital Treatment*, ed. L. A. Stein and M. A. Test (New York: Plenum Press, 1977), 75–113.

11. R. A. Fischer, "A Cartography of the Ecstatic and Meditative States," *Science* 174 (November 26, 1971): 897–904.

12. J. W. Perry, *Lord of the Four Quarters* (New York: Braziller, 1966; New York: Paulist Press, 1991); idem, *The Far Side of Madness*; idem, *Roots of Renewal*.

13. C. G. Jung, "Concerning Mandala Symbolism," in *The Archetypes and the Collective Unconscious*, trans. R. F. C. Hull, *Collected Works*, vol. 9, Bollingen Series XX, (Princeton, N.J.: Princeton University Press, 1959).

14. Ibid.

15. Paul, Romans 6:1–11.

16. Ibid.

17. Ibid.

18. Ibid.

Appendix C. Alternatives to Hospitalization

1. J. G. Gunderson, "Drugs and Psychosocial Treatment of Schizophrenia Revisited," *Journal of Continuing Education* (December 1977): 25–40.

2. C. G. Jung, *The Psychogenesis of Mental Disease, Collected Works*, vol. 3, Bollingen Series XX (New York: Pantheon, 1960).

3. J. W. Perry, "Reconstitutive Process in the Psychopathology of the Self," *Annals of the New York Academy of Sciences* 96 (1962): 853–76.

4. T. J. Scheff, *Being Mentally Ill* (Chicago: Aldine, 1966).

5. J. W. Perry, *The Far Side of Madness* (Englewood Cliffs, N.J.: Prentice Hall, 1974); idem, *Roots of Renewal in Myth and Madness*, (San Francisco: Jossey-Bass, 1976).

6. R. B. Berke, "Jungian-Oriented Residential Treatment for Schizophrenics at a State Hospital," *Hospital and Community Psychiatry* 30.8 (1979): 561–62.

Bibliography

Arieti, S. *Interpretation of Schizophrenia*. New York: Robert Brunner, 1955.

Barron, F. *Creativity and Psychological Health*. Princeton: Van Nostrand, 1963.

Bentzen, A. *Kina and Messiah*. London: Butterworth, 1955.

Bleuler, E. *Dementia Praecox or The Group of Schizophrenias*. Trans. J. Zinkin. New York: International Universities Press, 1950.

Bodde, D. "Harmony and Conflict in Chinese Philosophy." In *Studies and Thought in Chinese Philosophy*, ed. A. Wright. Chicago: University of Chicago Press, 1953.

Boisen, A. T. *The Exploration of the Inner World*. Chicago: Willett, Clark & Co., 1936.

Breasted, J. H. *The Dawn of Conscience*. New York: Charles Scribner, 1983.

Cameron, N. "Experimental Analysis of Schizophrenic Thinking." In *Language and Thought in Schizophrenia*, ed. J. S. Kasanin. Berkeley: University of California Press, 1944.

Cammann, S. V. R. "Suggested Origins of the Tibetan Mandala Painting," *Art Quarterly*, vol. 13. No. 2, Spring 1950.

Carpenter, W. T. and D. W. Heinrichs. "Treatment-Relevant Subtypes in Schizophrenia." *Journal of Nervous and Mental and Mental Disease* 169.2 (February 1981): 113–19.

Chang, K. C. *Art, Myth and Ritual*. Cambridge: Harvard University Press, 1983.

Childe, V. G. *New Light on the Most Ancient Near East*. New York: Grove Press, 1947.

———. *The Prehistory of European Society*. London: Penguin, 1974.

Chuang-Tse. "The Writings of Chuang-Tse." In *The Texts of Taoism*, ed. J. Legge. New York: Julian Press, 1959.

Confucius. *The Analects of Confucius*. Trans. A. Waley. New York: Vintage Books, Random House, 1938.

Creel, H. G. *The Birth of China*. New York: Frederick Ungar, 1937.

Dabrowski, K. *Postive Disintegration*. Boston: Little, Brown, 1986.

Danielou, A. *Shiva and Dionysus*. Trans. K. F. Hurry. New York: Inner Traditions International, 1984.

Davidson, H. R. E. *Gods and Myths of Northern Europe*. Baltimore: Penguin Books, 1964.

Deikman, A. "Bimodal Consciousness." *Archives of General Psychiatry* 45 (1971): 481–89.

Dossey, L. *Space-Time and Medicine*. Boulder, Colo.: Shambhala, 1982.

Dunbar, H. F. *Emotions and Bodily Changes*. New York: Columbia University Press, 1936.

Dundes, A. *The Flood Myth*. Berkeley: University of California Press, 1988.

Eliade, M. *Myth and Reality*. Trans. W. R. Trask. New York: Harper & Row, 1963.

———. *The Myth of the Eternal Return*.Trans. W. R. Trask. New York: Harper & Row, 1963.

Ellis, A. *Growth through Reason*. Palo Alto, Calif.: Science and Behavior Books, 1971.

Engel, G. L. "The Clinical Application of the Biopsychosocial Model." *American Journal of Psychiatry* 137.5 (1975): 535–44.

Enoch. *Book of Enoch*. Ed. R. Charles II. Los Angeles: Work of the Chariots, 1970.

Erickson, E. H. *Insight and Responsibility*. New York: Norton 1964.

Esdras. *The Aprocrypha*. Ed. M. Komroff. New York: Tudor, 1936.

Ferguson, M. *The Aquarian Conspiracy*. Los Angeles: Tarcher, 1980.

Fischer, R. "A Cartography of The Ecstatic and Meditative States." *Science* 174 (1971): 897–904.

Fitzgerald, C. P. *China*. New York: Praeger, 1961.

Foucalt, M. *Madness and Civilization*. New York: New American Library, Mentor Books, 1967.

Frankfort, H. *Kingship and the Gods: A Study of the Ancient Near Eastern Religion as the Integration of Society and Nature*. Chicago: University of Chicago Press, 1948.

Fung Yu-Lan. *A Short History of Chinese Philosophy*. Ed. D. Bodde. New York: Macmillan, 1960.

Gaster, T. H. *Thespis: Ritual, Myth and Drama in the Ancient Near East*. Garden City, N.J.: Doubleday, Anchor Books, 1961.

Gennep, A. Van. *The Rites of Passage*. Chicago: University of Chicago Press, 1960.

Girardot, N. J. "Behaving Cosmologically in Early Taoism." In *Cosmogony and Ethical Order*, ed. R. Lovin and F. E. Reynolds. Chicago: University of Chicago Press, 1985.

Gleik, J. *Chaos: Making a New Science*. New York: Viking, Penguin, 1987.

Goldstein, K. "Methodological Approaches to the Study of Schizophrenic Thought Disorder." In *Language and Thought in Schizophrenia*, ed. J. Kasanin. Berkeley: University of California Press, 1944.

Grof, S. *Beyond the Brain: Birth, Death and Transcendence in Psychotherapy*. Albany: State University of New York Press, 1985.

————. *Realms of the Human Unconscious: Observations from L.S.D. Research*. New York: E. P. Dutton, 1976.

Gunderson, J. G. "Drugs and Psychosocial Treatment Revisited," *Journal of Continuing Medical Education* (December 1977): 25–40.

Hesse, H. "Incipit Vita Nuova." In Stories of Five Decades, trans. R. Manheim, ed. T. Ziolkowski. London: Triad/Panther, 1976, pp. 41–42.

Hooke, S. H. *Myth and Ritual*. London: Oxford University Press, 1933.

————. Myth, *Ritual and Kinaship*. Oxford: Clarendon Press, 1958.

Jantsch, E. *The Self-Organizing Universe*. Oxford and New York: Pergamon Press, 1980.

Johnson, A. R. *Sacral Kingship in Ancient Israel*. Cardiff: University of Wales Press, 1955.

Jung, C. G. "The Association Method" (1910). In *Experimental Researches*. Trans. R. F. C. Hull. *Collected Works*, vol. 2. Bollingen Series XX. Princeton, N.J.: Princeton University Press, 1973.

————. "Commentary on the Secret of the Golden Flower" (1929). In *Alchemical Studies*. Trans. R. F. C. Hull. *Collected Works*, vol. 13. Bollingen Series XX. Princeton, N.J.: Princeton University Press, 1974.

————. "Concerning Mandala Symbolism" (1950). In *The Archtypes and the Collective Unconscious*. Trans. R. F. C. Hull. *Collected Works*, vol. 9. Bollingen Series XX. Princeton, N.J.: Princeton University Press, 1959.

————."The Content of The Psychoses" (1914). In *The Psychogenesis of Mental Disease*. Trans. R. F. C. Hull,. *Collected Works*, vol. 3. Bollingen Series XX. Princeton, N.J.: Princeton University Press, 1974.

―――. "Mind and Earth" (1931). In *Civilization in Transition*. Trans. R. F. C. Hull. *Collected Works*, vol. 10. Bollingen Series XX. Princeton, N.J.: Princeton University Press, 1959.

―――. *Mysterium Coniunctionis*. Trans. R. F. C. Hull. *Collected Works*, vol. 14. Bollingen Series XX. Princeton, N.J.: Princeton University Press, 1965.

―――. "On Psychic Energy" (1928). In *The Structure and Dynamics of the Psyhe*. Trans. R. F. C Hull. *Collected Works*, vol. 8. Bollingen Series XX. Princeton, N.J.: Princeton University Press, 1960.

―――. "On Psychological Understanding" (1914). In *The Psychogenesis of Mental Disease*. Trans. R. F. C. Hull. *Collected Works*, vol. 3. Bollingen Series XX. Princeton, N.J.: Princeton University Press, 1957.

―――. "On the Importance of the Unconscious in Psychopathlogy" (1914). In *The Psychogenesis of Mental Disease*. Trans. R. F. C. Hull. *Collected Works*, vol. 3. Bollingen Series XX. Princeton, N.J.: Princeton University Press, 1957.

―――. "On The Problem of Psychogenesis in Mental Disease" (1919). In *The Psychogenesis of Mental Disease*. Trans. R. F. C. Hull. *Collected Works*, vol. 3. Bollingen Series XX. Princeton, N.J.: Princeton University Press, 1957.

―――. *Psychology and Alchemy*. Trans. R. F. C Hull. *Collected Works*, vol. 12. Bollingen Series XX. Princeton, N.J.: Princeton University Press, 1955.

―――. The Psychology of Dementia Praecox" (1907). In *The Psychogenesis of Mental Disease*. Trans. R. F. C. Hull. *Collected Works*, vol. 3. Bollingen Series XX. Princeton, N.J.: Princeton University Press, 1957.

―――. "Schizophrenia" (1958). In *The Psychogenesis of Mental Disease*. Trans. R. F. C. Hull. *Collected Works*, vol. 3. Bollingen Series XX. Princeton, N.J.: Princeton University Press, 1959.

―――. *The Secret of the Golden Flower*. Trans. C. F. Baynes. London: Kegan Paul, Trench and Trubner, 1935.

―――. "Studies in Word Association" (1905–9). In *Experimental Researches*. Trans. R. F. C. Hull. *Collected Works*, vol. 2. Bollingen Series XX. Princeton, N.J.: Princeton University Press, 1965.

―――. *Symbols of Transformation*. Trans. R. F. C. Hull. *Collected Works*, vol. 5. Bollingen Series XX. Princeton, N.J.: Princeton University Press, 1956.

―――. *Two Essays on Analytical Psychology*. Trans. R. F. C. Hull. *Collected Works*, vol. 7. Bollingen Series XX. Princeton, N.J.: Princeton University Press, 1959.

―――. "Two Kinds of Thinking" (1912–56). In *Symbols of Transformation*. Trans. R. F. C. Hull. *Collected Works*, vol. 5. Bollingen Series XX. Princeton, N.J.: Princeton Unversity Press, 1956.

———. "The Transcendent Function" (1916–58). In *The Structure and Dynamics of the Psyche*. Trans. R. F. C. Hull. *Collected Works*, vol. 8. Bollingen Series XX. Princeton, N.J.: Princeton University Press, 1960.

Kasanin, J. S. "The Disturbance of Conceptual Thinking in Schizophrenia." In *Language and Thought in Schizophrenia*, ed. J. S. Kasanin. Berkeley: University of California Press, 1944.

Kerenyi, C. *Dionysus*. Bollingen Series LXV, vol. 2. Princeton, N.J.: Princeton University Press, 1975.

Klausner, J. *The Messianic Idea in Isreal*. Trans. W. F. Stienespring. New York: Macmillan, 1955.

Kris, E. *Psychoanalytic Explorations in Art*. New York: International University Press, 1952.

La Barre, W. "Materials For a History of Studies of Crisis Cults." *Current Anthropology* 12.1 (1971): 3–44.

Laing, R. D. and A. Esterson. *Sanity, Madness and the Family*. Baltimore: Pelican Books, 1970.

Lame Deer. *Lame Deer, Seeker of Visions*. Ed. R. Erdoes. New York: Washington Square Press, 1976.

Laternaari, V. *The Religions of The Oppressed*. New York: Mentor Books, New American Library, 1965.

Latourette, K. S. *The Chinese: Their History and Culture*. New York: Macmillan, 1946.

Leeper, R. W. "Motivational Theory of Emotion to Replace Emotion as Disorganizational Response." *Psychological Review* 55.1 (January 1948): 5–21.

Levene, H. I. "Acute Schizophrenia: Clinical Effects of the Labelling Process." *Archives of General Psychiatry* 25 (September 1971): 215–22.

Liberman, R. P. et al. "Drug-Psychosocial Interactions in The Treatment of Schizophrenia." In *The Chronically Mentally Ill: Research and Services*, ed. M. Mirabi. New York: Spectrum Publications, 1984.

Liddel and Scott. *An Intermediate Greek-English Lexicon*. New York: American Book Co., 1975.

Lin-Yutang. *The Wisdom of the East*. New York: Random House, 1942.

Locke, J. "Essay Concerning Human Understanding." In *Philosophical Works*. London: St. John, Ed., 1854.

Maslow, A. H. *The Farther Reaches of Human Nature*. New York: Viking, 1971.

Mencius. *The Four Books*. Trans. J. Legge. Shanghai: The Commercial Press.

Mosher, L. R. "Community Residential Treatment for Schizophrenia: 2 Year Followup." *Hospital and Community Psychiatry* 29 (1978): 715–23.

Mosher, L. R., R. J. Wendt, John Mathews, and A. Z. Menn. "Comparison of Two Enviroments for Schizophrenia." In *Principles and Practices of Milieu Therapy*, ed. J. G. Gunderson et al. New York: Jason Aronson, 1983.

Mosher, L. R. and A. Menn. "Lowered Barriers in the Community: The Soteria Model." In *Alternatives to Mental Hospital Treatment*, ed. L. A. Stein and M. A. Test. New York: Plenum Press, 1977.

Mowinkel, S. *He That Cometh*. Trans. G. W. Anderson. New York: Abingdon, 1954.

Needham, J. "Human Laws and the Laws of Nature in China and the West." *Journal of the History of Ideas* 12 (1951).

————. *Time: The Refreshing River*. London: Allen and Unwin, 1943.

Ornstein, R. E. *The Psychology of Consciousness*. San Francisco: W. H. Freeman, 1972.

Otto, R. *The Idea of The Holy*. London: Oxford University Press, 1950.

Otto, W. F. *Dionysus: Myth and Cult*. Trans. P. B. Palmer. Bloomington: Indiana University Press, 1965.

O'Shaughnessy, A. W. E. "Ode." In *The Oxford Book of Enqlish Verse*, ed. A. T. Quiller-Couch. Oxford: Clarendon Press, 1905.

Perry, J. W. "Emotions and Object Relations." *Journal of Analytical Psychology* 15.1 (1970): 1–12.

————. "Eros and History." *Anima* 3.1 (1976): 30–38.

————. *The Far Side of Madness*. Englewood Cliffs, N.J.: Prentice Hall, 1974; Dallas: Spring Publications, 1989.

————. *The Heart of History*. Albany: State University of New York Press, 1987.

————. *Lord of the Four Quarters*. New York: Braziller, 1966; New York: Paulist Press, 1991.

————. "Reconstitutive Process in the Psychopathology of the Self." *Annals of the New York Academy of Sciences* 96 (January 27, 1962): 853–76.

————. *Roots of Renewal in Myth and Madness*. San Francisco: Jossey-Bass, 1976.

————. *The Self in Psychotic Process*. Berkeley: University of California Press, 1953; Dallas: Spring Publications, 1987.

Plato. *Phaedrus*. In *The Dialogues of Plato*. Trans. B. Jowett. Oxford: Clarendon Press, 1871.

Prigogine, I. *Order Out of Chaos: Man's New Dialoque with Nature*. New York: Bantam Books, 1984.

Rappaport, M. et al. "Are There Schizophrenics for Whom Drugs May Be Unnecessary or Contraindicated?" *International Pharmacopsychatry* 13 (1978): 100–111.

Rhine, J. B. *Extra-Sensory Perception*. Boston, 1934.

Ring, K. *Heading toward Omega*. New York: Quill, Morrow, 1984.

———. *Life at Death*. New York: Quill, Morrow, 1982.

———. "Prophetic Visions in 1988: A Critical Reappraisal." *Journal of Near-Death Studies* 7 (1988): 4–18.

Rogers, C. *Client-Centered Therapy in Current Practice: Implications and Theory*. Boston: Houghton Mifflin, 1951.

Roszak, T. *Where the Wasteland Ends*. Garden City, N.J.: Doubleday, 1972.

Sandner, D. *Navaho Symbols of Healing*. New York: Harvest Books, Harcourt Brace and Jovanovich, 1979.

Scheff, T. J. *Being Mentally Ill*. Chicago: Aldine, 1966.

Shelley, P. B. *The Poetical Works of Percey Bysshe Shelley*. Ed. Mary Shelley. London: Edward Maxon, 1857.

Silverman, J. "Personality Trait and 'Perceptual Style': Studies of the Psychotherapists of Schizophrenic Patients." *Journal of Nervous and Mental Diseases* 145 (1967): 5–17.

———. "The Problem of Attention in Research and Theory in Schizophrenia." *Psychological Review* 71 (1964): 352–79.

Soothill, W. E. *The Hall of Light: A Study of Early Chinese Kingshp*. New York: Philosophical Library, 1952.

Sorokin, P. A. *The Crisis of Our Age*. New York: E. P. Dutton, 1942.

Sullivan, H. S. "The Language of Schizophrenia." In *Language and Thought in Schizophrenia*, ed. J. S. Kasanin. Berkeley: University of California Press, 1946.

Storch, A. "The Primitive and Archaic Forms of Inner Experience and Thought in Schizophrenia." *Journal of Nervous and Mental Disease*, Monograph Series No. 36, 1924.

Teilhard de Chardin, P. *The Phenomenon of Man*. New York: Harper & Row, 1965.

Thomas, E. J. *The Life of the Buddha as Legend and History*. New York: Barnes and Noble, 1960.

Tung Chung-Shu. "Ch'ien Ch'u Fan-Lu." Trans. B. Watson. In *Sources of Chinese Tradition*, ed. W. T. de Bary. New York: Columbia University Press, 1960.

Turneville-Petre, E. O. G. *Myth and Religion of the North*. New York: Rhinehart and Winston, 1964.

Vitgotsky, L. "Thought in Schizophrenia." *Archives of Neurology and Psychiatry* 31 (1934).

Waley, A. *The Way and Its Power*. New York: Grove Press, 1958.

Wallace, A. F. C. *Culture and Personality*. New York: Random House, 1970.

———. *The Death and Rebirth of the Seneca*. New York: Knoph, 1970.

———. "Stress and Rapid Personality Change." *International Record of Medical and General Practice Clinics* 169.12 (1956): 761, 744.

Waters, F. *The Masked Gods: Navaho and Pueblo Ceremonialism*. New York: Ballantine Books, 1950.

Webb, T. *Shelley: A Voice Not Understood*. Manchester, U.K.: Manchester University Press, 1977.

Wheatley, P. *The Pivot of the Four Quarters*. Chicago: Alden, 1971.

White, W. A. "The Language in Schizophrenia." In *Schizophrenia*. Association Research NMD. New York: Hoeber, 1928.

Worsley, P. *The Trumpet Shall Sound: A Study of Cargo Cults in Melanesia*. New York: Schoken Books, 1968. (2d Edition).

Yeats, W. B. *The Winding Stair and Other Poems*. New York: Macmillan, 1933.

Zarlock, S. P. "Societal Expectations, Language and Schizophrenia." *Journal of Humanistic Psychology* vol. 6, Spring 1966.

Index